Bad Girls of the Bible

Bad Girls of the Bible

EXPLORING WOMEN OF

QUESTIONABLE VIRTUE

BARBARA J. ESSEX

United Church Press
Cleveland, Ohio

United Church Press, Cleveland, Ohio 44115

© 1999 by Barbara J. Essex

04 03 02 01 00 99   5 4 3 2 1

Library of Congress Cataloging-in-Publication Data

Essex, Barbara J. (Barbara Jean), 1951–
    Bad girls of the Bible : exploring women of questionable virtue / Barbara J. Essex.
        p.   cm.
    ISBN 0-8298-1339-X (pbk. : alk. paper)
        1. Women in the Bible.   2. Bible Commentaries.   I. Title.
    BS575.E88   1999
    220.9'2'082—dc21   99-30818
                                                                          CIP

To "BAD GIRLS" EVERYWHERE:

YOU KNOW WHO YOU ARE!

CONTENTS

GETTING STARTED

*T*his study is designed for twelve weeks. The ideal length of time for each session is one and a half to two hours; feel free, however, to make adjustments that work for your group. You will need a Bible, this book, and a notebook or journal.

For individuals using this resource, you are encouraged to allot the same amount of time for each study. You, too, will need a Bible, this book, and a notebook or journal in which to record your reflections and questions.

At the end of the book, "Suggestions for Teaching and Preaching *Bad Girls of the Bible*" contains hints for using this resource in the church. The "Resources" section lists some books that will give more information about the texts than this volume can provide. You may want to include other materials that you find enlightening and inspirational.

Keep an open mind during this study, and have fun!

INTRODUCTION

Bad Girls of the Bible: Exploring Women of Questionable Virtue is a book for all adult believers. This volume is for women and men, laity and clergy, who seek fresh ways of preaching and teaching the stories of the Bible. Everybody has a story. Some are funny and make us glad. Others are depressing and make us sad. Some stories are more interesting than others; some should never be shared. But whether stories are happy or sad, we all have one. The preaching and teaching that we already do in church are nothing more than the sharing of stories—stories of the past and present with an eye toward the future.

Stories have the ability to shape and reshape our opinions. They have the capacity to confirm or challenge our stereotypes. There is a myth, for instance, that some men date "bad" girls and marry "good" ones. Therefore, women who are independent, thoughtful, and strong are often seen as "bad girls." They are not considered feminine, soft, and round; they are not considered good wife and mother material. They are labeled as cold, angular, callous, and cold-blooded. It is said that they take jobs from men when they should be home raising children. Young women are encouraged to be virgins until they marry. But no such expectations are placed on young men. Generally, men are encouraged to "sow their wild oats" and to get "it" out of their systems before they "settle down."

Not that long ago, men who did not marry were referred to as "swinging bachelors" while unmarried women were referred to as "old maids" or "spinsters." These terms are no longer widely used, but some attitudes implied by that language persist. Women are encouraged to create warm, loving homes and to raise healthy children. Men are encouraged to forge into the world and make their fortunes in order to provide financially for their families. Women have been taught to suppress themselves in order to make men comfortable—it is not good to be too smart, too strong, too wise. All of this is too threatening to some men. Unfortunately, there is nothing new about these attitudes and stereotypes. Images of weak women who need strong men to take care of them go back beyond the Bible.

Each year, I receive numerous invitations to deliver "Women's Day" sermons. For some time now, I have recycled the stories of a few biblical women that lend themselves to mostly positive conclusions. The exercise of finding fresh insights into the familiar stories of Hannah, Esther, Deborah, and Mary, mother of Jesus, has been challenging and stimulating as well as frustrating.

My determination to preach about good role models has had its reward. However, I found myself ignoring a whole group of biblical women. Even cursory examinations of their stories caused me to fear sharing them. What word of encouragement, inspiration, and redemption could I glean from Eve, who was cast out of paradise? Or Potiphar's wife, who falsely cried rape? Or Lot's wife, who was reduced to a lump of salt? Or Jezebel, who was thrown from a window and devoured by dogs? Or Sapphira, who was struck dead for stealing and lying?

It was easier, more positive, and more inspiring to preach about Hannah, whose unwavering practice of prayer is a model for all believers. It was more comforting to preach about Esther, who rose to heroic (or sheroic) heights despite her insecurities. It was more inspiring to preach about Deborah, who exhibited astonishing courage and military leadership. It was less troubling to preach about Mary, mother of Jesus, who selflessly risked her reputation to do God's bidding. These women had positive lessons to teach and could serve as role models for women and men as they worked for and with God to bring justice and hope and faith to God's people.

The task was easier, but these other women, the "bad" ones, would not remain silent. Whenever I searched again for Hannah, Eve was there. Whenever I reexplored Esther's story, Delilah was there. Whenever I reexamined Deborah's story, Gomer was there. Whenever I listened for a new word from Mary, Herodias was there. And so, the adventure began. I tentatively studied Eve, Delilah, Jezebel, and Gomer. It was rough going; the Bible does not give them much forgiveness. My early attempts were awkward as I tried to redeem them for the sake of leaving congregations with reasons to hope for a better life. I am afraid that my attempts were less than satisfying. I began to wonder if other things were impinging on their stories—things such as the theological perspective of the final writers of the biblical books and the functions of the women in salvation history. Once I began to dig a little deeper, I found nuggets of pure gold.

This book is about biblical women who have haunting stories of betrayal, jealousy, unfulfilled needs and dreams, deception, misunderstandings, rejection, exploitation, and sacrifice. It has been an intriguing exercise over the past three years to examine the lives of these "bad girls" of the Bible. Many of their stories are difficult to pinpoint; for the most part, their stories are included in larger stories of biblical men. Further, the biblical writers do not always provide enough information to get full portraits of them. For example, there is poor Mrs. Lot—her story consists of one verse: "But Lot's wife, behind him, looked back, and she became a pillar of salt" (Gen. 19:26). There is the story of Sapphira who, along with her husband, withheld some of the proceeds from a real estate deal. The custom in the early church community was to donate all moneys to a common fund designed to make sure that all members had the necessary resources for a good life. Without questioning her, God struck her dead on the spot (Acts 5)! We do not know very much about her life or her motives.

Many women in the Bible remain nameless. The stories of some women are difficult because God seems to condone their abuse, is absent, or remains silent. I have wished I could arbitrarily change the biblical witness to make the bad girls better. However, I do not have that prerogative; thus, many of the stories remain sad, unsatisfying, and unresolved.

Despite the difficulties, the journey has been exciting. There is much to be learned from and shared in their stories. Their stories convict the men in their lives who abuse and use them; their stories force us to think about social structures and systems; their stories impel us to look at ourselves and the roles women play in their own oppression and unhappiness. I invite you to join me on a path that is newly created. This volume, *Bad Girls of the Bible,* continues on the path paved by other feminist and womanist scholars. You will not be disappointed—God is not finished with us and speaks even in the stories of these bad girls. Their stories tell us about courage, determination, independence, and boldness. Their stories tell us about women who make the best choices they can with the knowledge and resources they have. Their stories tell us about women who are not so very different from ourselves.

As we question these women about their identities, motives, and assumptions, I hope we, too, female and male, are moved, compelled, and motivated to explore our own lives and stories. This is the effect that these bad girls have had on me. I am not ashamed to confess that they have pushed me to places I would rather not venture. Yet they have been comforting in their challenges. I am glad you have decided to join the adventure.

This book is written to be informative, user-friendly, and inspirational. It assumes that the reader has little or no prior knowledge of the technical aspects of biblical exegesis. This book consists of the following: an overview of biblical interpretative tools; Bible study units on selected "bad girls," each with an overview of the text and context, word studies where appropriate, and Reflection Questions; an overview of historical-critical methods; suggestions of ways to use this resource in the preaching and teaching of the local church; and a bibliography for further study.

We will get to know these women through nonthreatening study and thought-provoking Reflection Questions. This resource is manageable in the course of the church's life—twelve units that can be covered over a three-month period, or parts can be used for shorter study plans. Although other resources deal with recovering women's stories in the Bible, many tend to be scholarly and technical and are beyond the reach of laypersons who may not have a solid, historical-critical understanding of biblical interpretation.

It is my hope that *Bad Girls of the Bible* will be an easy and enjoyable resource for you. I want to challenge you, *and* I want you to have a good time!

This volume is a Bible study resource for adults that explores the stories of selected biblical women whose reputations are questionable. *Bad Girls of the Bible* is a twelve-week resource designed for individual, group, and retreat study. The women selected are well known even by persons who have little knowledge of the Bible; they include Eve, Delilah, Jezebel, and Herodias. These and other women are often denigrated and maligned in sermons and in the teaching of the church. In modern terms, they represent the so-called bad girls of the Scriptures. They are depicted as devious and despicable. Their stories are scattered throughout the Hebrew Scriptures (Old Testament) and Christian Scriptures (New Testament). Their stories are difficult to isolate because they are intertwined with the stories of powerful biblical men. However, recent scholarship is uncovering and recovering the voices of biblical women.

The current interest in women's stories and lives affirms that they are powerful despite being largely neglected and frequently distorted. The Bible helps to determine how women feel about themselves and how women are perceived in the world, and many of these perceptions are negative. Too often, the Bible categorizes women as very bad or very good; there is little in between these two extremes. Women in the Bible are primarily supports to the dominant male stories; the women show up just long enough to make a point, then they disappear. Some are named, but most women are not. A woman is known because she is a man's wife, mother, sister, or mistress. Women of the Bible are too often portrayed as failures.

This resource provides an alternative perspective on some biblical women. Rather than dismiss them as evil, this book attempts to give voice to the humanity of the women and highlight the difficulties of their situations. Further, this volume explores the positive character traits they exhibit in spite of the way in which they are depicted. In our exploration, we are seeking answers to important questions:

> Who are these women?
> What do their actions mean?
> Do their actions make them sinners or saints?
> What do their stories mean to us today?

Bad Girls of the Bible presents the stories of selected women from feminist and womanist perspectives because both take the lives and stories of women seriously and serve as a balance to the patriarchal view so pervasive in the Bible. *Bad Girls of the Bible* is a continuation of groundbreaking works such as

Just a Sister Away (Weems), *Helpmates, Harlots, and Heroes* (Bellis), and *To Love Delilah* (Cartledge-Hayes). They, along with others, began a process of recovering women's stories in the Bible from feminist and womanist perspectives—a process that was inevitable. These and similar works are the bases for this resource. However, this volume is a study resource for local church use by laypersons.

This resource combines biblical interpretative tools and gender studies to reveal a side of biblical women seldom reflected or considered in our preaching and teaching. For example, Delilah is blamed for the demise of Samson. However, when value judgments are lifted from her story (judgments that feed into the author's plan to show the heroics of Samson at the expense of Delilah), we find a woman who was independent, who exhibited entrepreneurial skills, who understood the power of her femininity and used it to her advantage. Similarly, Jezebel is dismissed as a truly evil person allegedly because she caused Israel to stray from God. Yet when value judgments are lifted from her story, we find that her zeal for her religion (which she practiced long before entering Israel's life) equaled Elijah's zeal for his religion. Further, Jezebel brought her royal background (she was a princess in a culture that provided royal prerogative) into her arranged marriage with Ahab, and her actions expressed a different understanding of privilege. There were, in essence, cultural differences and worldviews that seemed evil to Israel but were acceptable royal behavior in the culture at large.

Bad Girls of the Bible focuses directly on the women themselves within the context of Israel's life as well as the culture at large. This resource indicates how their stories fit into a larger theological understanding of history with its social, political, and economic implications. Even more, this volume shows these women as human beings with emotions, understandings, and challenges that people—especially women—today face. As far as is possible, negative value judgments and negative connotations have been lifted from their stories, and the women reveal who they are—despite what biblical writers attempt to portray.

Biblical stories are interesting, and those of women even more so. In many societies, women who speak boldly or make choices outside the norm of expectations are accused of being brash, aggressive, and shrill. The way language is used also influences perceptions of women. Women who misplace items are "dumb" females; men who are forgetful are "absent-minded." Women who deal with many men are "tramps," "sluts," or "loose women"; men who have intimate relationships with many women are called "womanizers." Women who understand the power of their femininity and use it to their advantage are considered shameless; men who are confident are praised.

Women who take faith and Bible study seriously may face a dilemma. On the one hand, the Bible shows a God who is concerned for the oppressed, and a Jesus who defied the cultural assumptions about women by interacting with them in meaningful ways. On the other hand, the Bible also portrays women as inferior and subordinate to men. While many biblical men have entire chapters and books devoted to their stories, most women get a verse or two. With the exception of a few women, most are seen in order to make a point, and we never see or hear from them again. Women of the Bible are too often known for negative reasons: they deceived their husbands, they made foolish choices, they defied the God of Israel, they got caught in sexual acts, and they seduced God's chosen people.

In spite of the Bible's ambivalence in its portrayal of women, many women have powerful experiences of God's grace and love as well as the comfort of Jesus' presence in their lives. Experience tells women they are cherished and worthy of love. A dualism in Christianity is the foundation for women's dilemma. God teaches women that they are created in God's image and likeness and, thus, should love themselves; and Jesus affirms the worth of women by the quality of his interaction with them throughout his life and ministry. However, the Bible teaches women to despise themselves. The Bible portrays numerous women in very negative tones: Job's wife was a foolish woman because she questioned the goodness and justice of God; Lot's wife was turned into a pillar of salt because she dared to look back on her past; the list goes on!

For many women, faith creates a conflict. The options for women are difficult ones: deny and ignore the dualism; address it and learn from it; or leave the faith. A growing number of women are choosing to leave the church because of the way women are treated—in the Bible and in society. They refuse to be castigated from the pulpits and in the classrooms of our churches. Fortunately, things are changing. More women are attending seminaries and pursuing biblical studies. Their efforts are providing new hope for those women who feel abused by the teachings of some churches.

The problem begins with the fact that the Bible is a difficult book! In some places, it reads like a dramatic piece with interesting characters and suspenseful plots. In other places, it reads like a poem with flowing rhythms and lofty images. In still other places, it reads like a history book recounting an endless list of dates and events. And in yet other places, it reads like a Census Bureau report listing family names with intimidating pronunciations. The Bible is filled with unfamiliar images, obscure language, repetitions, contradictions, and confusing time lines. While there is a method to the madness, the method is not readily apparent. It is not always easy to isolate the theological meanings of texts, and we may be lost in the confusion. In addition, when texts are lifted from their context, we may be even more confused by the seeming contradictions in the texts.

The Bible is composed of words—chosen by human beings who have been shaped and influenced by the culture within which they live and work. Words and their meanings change over time and are shaped by events of particular eras. The same holds true for the words of biblical texts. To compound the challenge, the Bible was not originally written in English. The Hebrew, Aramaic, and Greek languages lose much in translation and often confuse us because we miss the nuances of the words. Therefore, we must work hard to understand what the Bible means. We can do this through the tools of critical methods of interpretation. Such study can be tedious and overwhelming. Fortunately, others have done the hard work of biblical interpretation, and we need only take advantage of their scholarship.

Despite their attempts at objectivity, however, all biblical interpreters have been influenced by their times. Such influence is inevitable; it should not keep us from using the resources at our disposal. The Bible is a valuable source of life and faith for us. The Bible is able to address our present experiences of anxieties and hope. The Bible is the witness to God's power and grace in past generations and continues to be an expression of faith shared by a community still living today all over the world. Rather than shy away from the dilemma that the Bible presents for women, our challenge is to address the dilemma and learn from it.

The Old Testament, also known as the Hebrew Scriptures, was written in Hebrew (except for parts of Daniel, Ezra, and one verse in Jeremiah written in Aramaic). The New Testament, also known as the Christian Scriptures, was written in Greek. When we read the Bible, we are reading materials that have been translated into English. You are encouraged to use the version of the Bible with which you feel most comfortable. I will be using the New Revised Standard Version (NRSV) of the Bible. I will highlight Hebrew and Greek words when doing so sheds light on our understanding of the text.

The Bible was not written to be a history book as we have been taught to understand history. The Bible is more like a divine drama that speaks to us. It is a message about how God deals with human beings. The Bible reflects God's action in creation: God is the Creator, the Author and Finisher of this story and of our faith. The story of God's dealings with humankind is diverse because God is experienced in many ways. Therefore, we should not be surprised that the Bible reflects that same diversity: different authors, different historical situations, and different kinds of theological expressions and concerns.

The Bible is the most quoted and misquoted book ever written. It has been used over the years to oppress and exploit persons. The Bible has been quoted to keep African Americans submissive and enslaved. The Bible has been used to oppress and dominate women. Even today, the Bible is quoted to keep women out of the ministry and leadership roles in church and society. The Bible has been used to oppose and oppress persons of other faiths. The Bible is quoted to explain why other religions are inadequate and inferior to Christianity. The Bible has been quoted to justify war, destruction, and conquest. The Bible has been used to exclude and persecute gay men and lesbian women. The Bible has been used to rationalize the maintenance of a class of poor people. Each instance of oppression is justified because "it says so in the Bible." By using historical-critical Bible study methods, we hope to uncover deeper meanings of the texts, so that persons are affirmed rather than condemned.

The great irony is that the God of our Bible condemns injustice completely. If one were to read the Bible from Genesis to Revelation, one would experience a panoramic view of God's dealings with humanity. The Bible speaks of survival, deliverance, liberation, love, and community. God is committed to justice and freedom; God is on the side of weak, helpless, oppressed, and enslaved people. Serious study is needed to unlock the Bible. To gain a fuller understanding of the Bible, one needs to know something about languages, history, politics, geography, and culture. Modern research has made available some tools that enhance the study of the Bible. Without these tools, one is likely to read one's own opinions, biases, and thoughts into the Bible. (For an overview of these research tools, see the Resources section at the back of the book.)

The tools for biblical interpretation are complex and technical. The various methods overlap and are interdependent. The most important task for serious students of the Bible is to ask the following questions:

> Who "wrote" this book?
> What does the text say?
> Who was the intended audience for this message?
> What did this passage mean to the original audience?
> How did the meaning change over time and under different circumstances?
> What are the historical, political, social, and theological backgrounds for this passage?
> What does this passage mean to and for us today?

The Bible is a collection of ancient oral and written traditions that were edited into a whole over a long period of time. The traditions were expressed in stories, poems, lists, songs, and proverbs. Over time, they were refined and modified as circumstances for Israel changed. The traditions were expanded, written down, and edited to fit new situations. Several traditions in the Hebrew Scriptures are traceable primarily by the names used for God.

The earliest tradition is the Yahwist, or J. In Hebrew, the name for God is designated YHWH (*Yahweh* is the holy name that is not to be spoken in vain).

This symbolical rendering of the holy name is called the tetragrammaton, for the four Hebrew letters used as a biblical proper name for God. In our English Bibles, YHWH is designated as "LORD" or "LORD God." (Note that throughout this book, the word "Lord" has been replaced with "God" to avoid the male-gendered and hierarchical connotations of "Lord.") The Yahwist tradition is most evident in the book of Genesis. It is marked by vivid scenes, uses a lot of dialogue, shows an understanding of human nature, and uses anthropomorphisms. Anthropomorphism is ascribing human motivation, characteristics, or behavior to nonhuman things—in this case, God. For example, in Genesis, we are told that God "speaks" directly to human beings and that God "walks" in the garden.

The Elohist, or E, tradition supplements J but is more difficult to recognize. It uses the name Elohim for God before Moses' encounter with God. *Elohim* is a generic word that means "god[s]," and it appears in our Bibles as "God." The E tradition begins with Abraham, who is presented as a prophet. The E tradition avoids more obvious anthropomorphisms. God "speaks" generally through dreams, from clouds, in the midst of fire, or through mediums and angels. E reacts negatively to the other religions surrounding Israel; we will detect some hostility toward other faiths, including the worship of Baal.

The Deuteronomic history, or D tradition, is found mostly in the book of Deuteronomy, and its influence extends from Deuteronomy to Second Kings. It emphasizes the relationship between God and humankind. It has a style that encourages or urges Israelites to good deeds. The language points to a period of religious crisis. One such period followed the collapse of Israel when the Assyrian threat to Judah continued and a number of evil kings endangered *Yahwist* religion. D asserts that salvation could be had by exhibiting a loyal response to God's covenant laws and by returning to pure worship of God at Jerusalem. The basic theme of D is that the judgment of Israel was due to the serious sins of the people; the judgment was justified and explained to the people so that they would change their ways and return to obedience to God's law.

The Priestly, or P, tradition was shaped by the priests of Jerusalem and emphasizes a concern for liturgy. The P materials are primarily religious and legal documents. P reworks J and E materials to reflect the point of view of the Jerusalem priesthood with its various rituals and regulations. The tradition originates during the time of Moses and gets its authority from the revelation on top of Mount Sinai. P's style is abstract and redundant. This tradition uses a lot of genealogies. It is concerned with chronological correctness and gives very detailed descriptions of rituals and procedures. It avoids anthropomorphisms. The major theme of this tradition is that as God is holy, so must Israel remain holy. Israel must separate itself from and remain uncontaminated by any human-made cult or morality. P explains procedures for ritual and legal cleanness, such as those in the book of Leviticus.

The Redactor, or R, tradition is a way of talking about redaction criticism. "Redaction" is the manner in which biblical texts were edited. The Redactor wove various stories together into a new understanding that reflected a change in context. Redaction criticism has been helpful in our understanding of the Christian Scriptures. We know through other means of biblical criticism and archaeological findings that Mark is the earliest Gospel. Both Matthew and Luke used Mark as a foundation for their Gospels. However, both Matthew and Luke added to and reinterpreted various stories and incidents in Mark. That was not an uncommon practice, and it is done today. The changes they made reflected their larger purposes as well as the changing needs of their communities. Preachers redact texts in order to make a point about God's activity in the world today. The Redactor helps us to see a bigger theological picture as circumstances change and are analyzed in view of God's purposes for creation.

No doubt this brief overview of traditions and sources makes little sense now, but having some idea of them will help to unpack the texts when we study the individual women. For instance, it will help to know that Elijah was so fierce in his pursuit to destroy the priests of Baal because exclusive belief in God was required for faithfulness. Further, it will help to know why the Bible strongly opposes Israelites' marriages to foreign women. The traditions will help us see the bigger picture when we examine selected stories and characters. These traditions give shape to how women were perceived in ancient Israel. Along with biblical interpretative tools, we will need some idea of how we are approaching the stories of these "bad girls." The predominant framework for the perception of women in the Bible is called patriarchy. However, we will look at our bad girls through the lenses of feminism and womanism.

"Patriarchy" is the system that sets up the legal mechanisms in the society and makes male dominance over women and children a part of that system. It means that men hold the power in the important institutions of society and that women are to be denied access to such power. Patriarchy does not imply that women are completely helpless or powerless. With some exceptions, the roles for women are clearly defined and are often limited. For ancient Israel, aspects of patriarchy include the understandings that the family is the basic unit and is headed by a father; that family history is traced through the father's bloodlines; that the wife moves into the husband's house; that women's roles are primarily those of wife and mother, especially mother of male children. For those in Israel, there were harsh penalties for sexual transgressions, and the punishment for women was harsher. Likewise, there were harsh penalties for nonexclusive worship of God. Thus, Jezebel is portrayed as evil personified because she dared to believe in a god other than Israel's God.

In a patriarchal society, women are givers, not takers. They sacrifice for their men and children. There are exceptions; some women behave as men do, and the details of their stories are enlightening. Yet the ideal woman is mother rather than one who is independent and/or seductive.

Jesus carried out his ministry in a society marked by patriarchy. However, Jesus boldly affirmed the worth of women by interacting freely with them. Women were among his closest friends, and many women followed him. Jesus' relationships with and to women often placed him in conflict with the leaders of the Temple. For instance, the young woman caught in the act of adultery was brought before Jesus. The usual punishment for such an offense was stoning. But the man with whom she was caught was not brought forth with her. It is impossible for a woman to commit adultery alone! Yet the leaders did not bring her partner before Jesus.

In contrast to patriarchy, "feminism" is the perspective in which women are understood to be fully human and thus entitled to equal rights and privileges. Women are not considered subordinate or inferior to men. Feminism declares that women are marginalized automatically because the society is structured to support and affirm men. Feminist biblical interpreters seek to analyze other ancient cultures in order to isolate and affirm women's value. A feminist perspective works toward reclaiming and reconstructing stories of biblical women. It says that women's experiences are real and relevant. Feminism sees God as an important character in the biblical story. Further, feminism claims a voice for voiceless and silent women. By uncovering women's stories, feminist biblical interpreters highlight Jesus' explicit affirmation of women and break through the stereotypes of women in the Bible.

The issues of culture, status, and class are important in our understanding of the Bible. Some biblical interpreters feel that feminism does not adequately deal with these issues in interpretation. Thus, another perspective is needed. "Womanism" is a term created by Alice Walker, an African American female writer, to describe a theological and interpretative perspective that is inclusive rather than exclusive. A womanist is more than an African American feminist interpreter; a womanist is one who recognizes the humanity of all God's people, regardless of race, gender, class, or sexual orientation. A womanist perspective recognizes and celebrates boldness, independence, audacity, courage, emotion, freedom, strength, survival, commitment, faith, and hope. Womanism is concerned with survival in an unpredictable and uncertain world; it revisits biblical stories for women we can recognize and a God we can trust.

For example, womanism sees in the Hagar story the struggles and triumphs of all women, especially women of color. Hagar, an Egyptian slave woman used as a surrogate mother and cast out of the community, is symbolic of God's mercy and care for "foreign women" and for those victimized even by God's chosen ones—Abraham and Sarah. Sexual and economic exploitation, surrogacy, rape, domestic violence, alienation—all play a role. Womanism raises issues of authority, suffering, obedience, liberation, reconciliation, and power. These significant issues and themes emerge in the stories of the bad girls. Womanism provides a way of hearing their stories that does not leave them helpless victims.

The three concepts—patriarchy, feminism, and womanism—will be focal points as we attempt to cast the bad girls into lights where we can see them more clearly for the human beings they are. Our focus on uncovering the women's stories will be guided by the following questions:

> What is the background of the biblical women?
> What patriarchal functions do their stories serve?
> Concerning "foreign women," what did the women give up to be with Israelite men? What did they hope to gain by being with Israelite men?
> What character traits do the biblical women exhibit?
> How do the stories of biblical women coincide with feminist and/or womanist experiences?

We will not be able to answer all of these questions; some of our answers will be unsatisfactory. The point is to try to uncover as much as we can and recognize that there is much to be learned in the process.

Much of what we know about women's status in ancient Israel is found in the laws and stories in the Hebrew Scriptures. Most ancient cultures in that part of the world assumed patriarchy, polygamy, concubinage, slavery, and a double standard—one for men and another for women.

The basic social unit in Hebrew society was the family, headed by the father. The religious community was made up of adult males and warriors who were all circumcised and were designated as the "people of Israel." This understanding of community shaped the laws to preserve the wholeness of the family and to define the place of women, children, and foreigners.

There is evidence that women played many roles within the society: female prophets, seers, sages, judges (military leaders in the period before Israel lived under kings), queen mothers, entrepreneurs, farmers, and shepherds, among others. Yet their primary role was to bear children, preferably male children, for their husbands. Given the importance of the family and the father's bloodline, it is not surprising that adultery by married women was punishable by death. Adultery by the husband was not considered a crime unless he transgressed with a married woman. Men were permitted to have numerous wives and concubines. Brides were to be virgins; if not, they were to be executed. Prostitution was tolerated, but female prostitutes were considered outcasts. Divorce was practiced, but with a few exceptions, only men could seek divorce.

Property was usually passed from father to son; if there were no sons, then daughters inherited the property but were required to marry within the clan.

Before marriage, a woman was dependent on her father; after marriage, on her husband. If the husband died and there were no children, the property reverted to his clan or tribe. In some cases, widows were mated with brothers-in-law to obtain heirs for the dead husband. Usually, a widow was expected to return to her father's house (we will see both instances in Tamar's story). Not all widows could do that, however; thus, the prophets expressed concern for the well-being and support of widows, orphans, and various sojourners.

Only men could be priests. Only men were required to attend three annual pilgrim feasts. Women were frequently excluded from participation in feasts and Temple events due to "ritual uncleanness" associated with menstruation and childbirth. Women were to observe a period of impurity after childbirth—seven days for the birth of a son; fourteen for the birth of a daughter, implying that giving birth to girls was more ritually unclean than giving birth to boys! Imagine what this did to girls' self-esteem.

The lives of women after the monarchy (when Israel lived under kings like the other nations, starting with the reign of Saul) were especially difficult. The society set forth very negative attitudes against foreign women; we find evidence of this in various texts. Some commentators state that the real objection to marriages to foreign women was more economic and political than religious and ethnic. The issue was about the loss of inherited land, which points to women's greater legal rights because in Israel, only men could inherit land.

The stories of women and men in the Bible are interpretations by storytellers who left out some important details and embellished others. When distortion was necessary to make a point, storytellers distorted the story. Women are seen as threatening and dangerous creatures who need to be controlled or destroyed. Women's stories and experiences are ignored or treated with disdain. The message is that women are to be feared. However, when we are courageous enough to name the stereotypes and confront the myths about women in the Bible, we find not wicked women, but human beings— thinking, breathing, living women in tough situations who made the best choices they could at the time.

Though biblical women's stories have been distorted and are often used against women, the lives of these women represent the struggle for wholeness and dignity. Although cast as "bad girls," biblical women are more like us than they are different. They seek love, kindness, and hope; they are victims of envy, jealousy, and fear. We do well to recognize the cultural context of biblical stories and the limitations of that context. It is tempting to read contemporary values into the ancient stories. We must resist that temptation and be aware that biblical texts do not always give coherent or logical pictures of the characters and their struggles and triumphs. The biblical characters—female and male—will not always behave in the ways that we would want them to behave. We must withhold judgment and try to let them speak for themselves.

Despite the difficulties, the Bible provides a word of good news for women. The Bible, when read from different perspectives, can be the source of inspiration and comfort for women and men. When we earnestly study the Bible, we find women in a multitude of roles: mothers—wed and unwed; wives; daughters; military and political leaders; prophets and sages; disciples; deacons and pastors; friends; loyal and religious persons. We find ourselves reflected in their stories, and we celebrate their joys and triumphs, their courage and dedication. We learn from their tragedies and despair, their pains and sorrows. We are blessed when we critique the traditions that hurt women, and we rejoice that God is still in our midst—working to make us whole.

1

EVE: WILLFUL OR WISE?

*T*he story of Eve plunges us immediately into the difficulties of under-standing the Bible. Her story is troubling because it sets the tone for the treatment of women throughout the ages. She is accused of disobeying God's command, and that act resulted in humanity's fall from grace. Her story is embedded in the larger story of creation. It is a long and complex story; we need to work through the texts to find her story and its related issues.

Some want the creation story to be historical, factual, and literal. In other words, they want it to be real. However, we are confronted with a challenge right off the bat. The creation story is actually two stories, neither of which was written by the first human beings. Scholars generally agree that Genesis 1–3 was probably shaped during the exilic period of Israel's history—thou-sands of years after the act of creation. In all probability, the Israelites did not talk or write about creation until after they had experienced some highs and lows: emancipation from Egyptian slavery and oppression; wanderings in the wilderness; a period of conquest, threat, and deliverance; a golden age under the leadership of David and Solomon; subsequent instability of other mon-archs; and finally, the devastation of Babylonian and Assyrian exile. Through all of their trials and triumphs, the Israelites believed that God was present in their history—God intervened on their behalf and allowed them to live the consequences of their decisions and choices. Given the reality of their expe-riences, the people would naturally ask some serious questions: What kind of God is our God? What makes our God different from other gods? Their responses varied over the years and generations, but central to their faith was the belief that their *God, in the beginning, created the heavens and the earth!*

Like all peoples, they sought to make sense of their world and their expe-riences within a faith system where God had made the divine presence known to them in concrete ways. The God of the Israelites was not a remote figure away in the heavens unconcerned about them. Rather, this God was knowable and accessible. This God talked to them and listened to them. This God fought their battles and made a way for them when no way was to be seen. This God loved them and sought communion with them. This God also punished them when they left the path made for them. This God was personal and involved in their lives. This God was like a parent, always seeking a balance between guidance and freedom.

There is little doubt that the Israelites knew of other creation stories—every culture has them as each tries to make sense of the world and to distinguish the culture's gods from other gods. In Genesis we have Israel's concepts of God.

Volumes have been written about how our universe came into being. Some believe that only God could create the diversity we experience: rivers, lakes, and streams; mountains, prairies, swamps, and deserts; giraffes, aardvarks, rhinoceroses, elephants, and coyotes; trout, shrimp, snails, and jellyfish; peaches, pomegranates, and papayas; roses, peonies, and dandelions; oak trees, maple trees, and palm trees; garlic, onions, and jalapeños; and the list goes on.

Others believe that all of creation happened with the accidental collision of rocks in space. Still others believe that life started from a single cell that evolved and differentiated into the world we experience today. Much has been written from both ends of the spectrum and everything in between.

We cannot know with scientific certainty how any of this world came to be. But we can and do know that something happened. As people of faith, we believe that God brought forth all that has been, all that is, and all that will be. How we express this belief is the crux of the matter at hand.

In Genesis, we have Judeo-Christian foundational theology: in the beginning, before anything was, there was God. God spoke creative words, and things came into being: light, night, sky, earth, seas, vegetation, sun, stars, living creatures—on earth and in the seas—and human beings. God said,

> "Let us make humankind in our image, according to our likeness." . . .
> So God created humankind in God's image,
> in the image of God, God created them;
> male and female God created them.
>
> God blessed them, and God said to them, "Be fruitful and multiply, and fill the earth and subdue it; and have dominion over . . . everything that has the breath of life." . . . And it was so. God saw everything that God had made, and indeed, it was very good. And there was evening and there was morning, the sixth day. (Gen. 1:26–31)

For years, Bible scholars have differentiated two creation stories. The first one, Genesis 1:1–2:3, is said to be of the P (Priestly) tradition. The God of Israel is One who speaks the universe into being. This God also affirms the divine handiwork—it was good!

On the sixth day, God creates humankind. God's speech here differs from that which brought forth other aspects of creation; here God says, "Let us make humankind in our image, according to our likeness" (Gen. 1:26). Some scholars believe that the "us/our" refers to some kind of heavenly court or assembly. Who they are and how they came to be are questions we have no answers for; they appear without explanation. It would appear that God had the experience of interacting and consulting with others before the creation of human beings. God was not alone in the beginning. What roles this divine assembly or council played are not given; we do not know who they were or what they did other than give advice to God. At any rate, God creates humankind—male and female—in God's image and likeness. The two words "image" (Hebrew *selem*) and "likeness" (Hebrew *demut*) convey the totality and concreteness of humankind's similarity to God. In mind, body, and spirit, humanity is like God. In a real sense, humankind has the potential for creativity, collaboration, concern, compassion, and action. It also means that humankind has the potential for achieving balance between work and rest (the seventh day was a day of rest).

After creating humankind in male and female forms, God blesses them and declares a twofold commandment: (1) be fruitful and multiply; and (2) subdue the earth and have "dominion" over fish, birds, and every living thing. The responsibility for human reproduction and creation now belongs to humankind. Male and female are to care for creation. The word translated "dominion" carries the meaning of taking care of something, not exploiting or abusing it. Male and female are created to be equal partners in work and life. Neither is designated superior or inferior; neither is to have dominion over the other. Their command is to work together as equals. The P tradition highlights the orderliness of creation, its goodness, and the equality of male and female in the created order.

The second creation story, Genesis 2:4–25, gives us another perspective on God's activity. Here, in the beginning, the earth is without water, without life of any kind. A stream rises from the earth; it is not clear whether this is at God's initiative. The first explicit act of creation is the forming of the *adam* (earth creature) from the dust. This earth creature is given a generic name; at this point, it is not the proper name of the one we call Adam. The word *adam* is most likely used in a generic sense, at least until Genesis 4:25, when it is used as a proper noun. Scholars are split on whether it is a proper noun in Genesis 2:20 and 3:17, 21. The *adam* remains lifeless until God performs CPR and breathes life into it. The second explicit act of creation is the planting of a garden called Eden. The *adam* is placed in the garden. The *adam*'s task is to till and keep the garden. The earth creature is to take care of it and bring forth its full potential. The first human being, according to the J (*Yahwist*) tradition, is to be a farmer, working the land until it blossoms (Gen. 2:4–9, 15).

In the midst of this gorgeous garden, God places two special trees: the tree of life and the tree of the knowledge of good and evil. Then God gives the *adam* a command: "You may freely eat of every tree of the garden; but of the tree of the knowledge of good and evil you shall not eat, for in the day that you eat of it, you shall die" (Gen. 2:16–17).

God speaks to the *adam* and permits the consumption from every tree (including the tree of life, it seems!) except the tree of the knowledge of good and evil. God both gives and withholds. The *adam* alone receives the command. There is no evidence that God and the *adam* discuss the command; it is given, and presumably, the *adam* accepts it. In this text, the *adam* is confronted with the possibility of death. Some biblical scholars see death in this text as something other than physical death. Death is as much a part of God's created order as life is. It has been suggested that death means more like the disintegration of the *adam*'s (and subsequent humans') relationship with God and the entire created order. That is, the *adam* has the freedom to choose—to eat or not to eat. Even in paradise, there are choice and limit. If the *adam* decides not to eat, it remains in right relationship with God, the boundaries of Creator and creature fully intact. The implication is that such boundaries are good because the creature is wholly dependent on God. The *adam*'s responsibilities are normal and natural; it fulfills its tasks gladly and willingly.

If the *adam* chooses to eat, however, it risks destroying the relationship with the Creator. To eat would be a declaration of independence that is a problem for the Creator—it would mean that the creature has moved outside the circle of trust that the Creator has developed. The decision of what to do with the tree of the knowledge of good and evil is clearly the *adam*'s. The earth creature has not spoken yet; we presume its silence is consent to the command.

As God surveys God's handiwork, God sees creation as incomplete: "It is not good that the *adam* should be alone; I will make it a helper as its partner" (Gen. 2:18).

It is not clear whether God speaks to the earth creature; God may be talking to the divine assembly introduced in Genesis 1:26. God seems to be saying that the *adam* needs more than God's presence. So, God experiments with providing a helper. The Hebrew that is translated as "helper" is *ezer*, from a root word meaning "help" or "support" and, by extension, "helper." The word does not carry the implication that the helper is subordinate or inferior to the one being helped (see Fretheim essay listed in the Resources section). God presents to the *adam* a procession of living creatures. The *adam* names them, but an appropriate helper has not been presented. The text does not clarify whether it is God or the *adam* that decided none of the living creatures is suitable. At any rate, God goes back to the drawing board and tries again in dramatic fashion: "So God caused a deep sleep to fall upon the *adam*, and it slept; then God took one of its ribs and closed up its place with flesh. And the rib that God had taken from the *adam* God made into a woman and brought her to the *adam*" (Gen. 2:21–22).

God creates woman; the *adam* is unconscious and unaware of God's creative work until it is finished. Woman, as helper, is not given a status of inferiority. God creates her, the same as the *adam*. She is created from the *adam*'s rib; the *adam*'s rib is created from dust; thus, both of their ultimate origins are rooted in the dirt. By God's initiative, both are created— neither is better than the other. Both are created beings having God's breath of life within them.

The order of their creation does not explicitly imply rank or status. Being created first does not make the object better than any created later. In Genesis 1:4–5, day is not better than the animals created in Genesis 1:20–21. All are part of God's creative process.

At this point, the *adam*'s speech is recorded, and what a declaration the *adam* utters:

> This at last is bone of my bones
> and flesh of my flesh;
> this one shall be called Woman,
> for out of Man this one was taken. (Gen. 2:23)

Renita Weems, renowned scholar of the Hebrew Scriptures who brings a womanist perspective, suggests that the *adam*'s declaration is the first love song in the Bible (see p. 12 of Moyers book listed in Resources). He expresses his wonder and joy at finally having a suitable companion. Both man and woman are inextricably connected, complementary, and share the same essence. The man's love song recognizes the difference between male and female, but does not imply superiority. The Hebrew words for "man" and "woman" share a common root word; they are the same, yet different, implying that both are equal. They do not oppose each other; together, they make a whole greater than either does individually. They are to work together as partners.

In both the P and the J traditions, God is accessible to and involved with the created order. Man and woman are commanded to continue God's creative process on the earth by nurturing creation. They are seen as equal and willing partners in this enterprise. God trusts them to carry out their duties. God and human beings work together; the rest of creation depends on the human beings to care for it. God is active, inventive, and imaginative. God is willing to take risks and extend the divine image and likeness to the human beings. God provides a wide range of freedom, yet maintains an appropriate boundary. God establishes a relationship of interdependence and mutuality with the human beings. God is both near and appropriately distant; there is no indication that God attempts to micromanage creation once the tasks are given to the human beings. They are free to govern creation as they see fit. God is willing to let the human beings take care of business, as it were. Thus, the future is open-ended. Neither God nor the human beings can know how things will turn out. What the human beings do will make a difference. There is great tension in this scenario, for the future is unpredictable.

The writer ends the creation story on a happy note—the man and the woman are in perfect harmony with each other, with God, and with the created order. All is well: "The man and his wife were both naked, and were not ashamed" (Gen. 2:25).

We are left in a state that is almost too good to be true! And our suspicions turn out to be right on. The scene in Genesis 3 opens with a theological discussion between the woman and the serpent:

> Now the serpent was more crafty than any other wild animal that God had made. He said to the woman, "Did God say, 'You shall not eat from any tree in the garden'?" The woman said to the serpent, "We may eat of the fruit of the trees in the garden; but God said, 'You shall not eat of the fruit of the tree that is in the middle of the garden, nor shall you touch it, or you shall die.'" But the serpent said to the woman, "You will not die; for God knows that when you eat of it your eyes will be opened, and you will be like God, knowing good and evil." So when the woman saw that the tree was good for food, and that it was a delight to the eyes, and that the tree was to be desired to make one wise, she took of its fruit and ate; and she also gave some to her husband, who was with her, and he ate. (Gen. 3:1–6)

The shift from creation to this text is sudden. The conversation flows as if it were a normal occurrence for the human beings to talk with the animals in the garden. We are told that the serpent is more crafty than other animals. It is not depicted as evil or wicked or bad. The human beings do not seem afraid or concerned. Why the serpent speaks only to the woman is not known. We do not know how the serpent knows what it knows. We cannot tell from the text whether the serpent overheard God's command to the *adam* or whether the serpent has eaten from the tree. It simply knows something the human beings do not. The serpent poses a question to the woman. (The way in which a question is posed shapes the answer given.) The serpent does not ask the woman about the range of freedom God had provided for her and the man. Instead, it asks about the limits to that freedom. A curious point is that the serpent addresses the woman rather than the man to whom the command was given. Her response is interesting—she cannot give a definite yes or no.

She knows the answer, even though she was not present when God handed the command to the man. Apparently, he relayed this information to her. We do not know what exactly he said; her response is not entirely accurate according to the earlier text.

She does not identify the tree as that of the knowledge of good and evil. She states that she and the man should not eat the fruit of the tree in the middle of the garden; nor are they allowed to even touch it or they will die. She seems to accept God's command as she understands it. She does not add her thoughts or unwillingness to comply; she seems to accept the reality as presented to her. She does not question its validity or her and the man's ability to obey the command.

Having set the stage to raise doubt about God in the woman's mind, the serpent continues. It tells her that God has lied to them—they will not die. Rather, God has withheld the truth from them because God wants to keep the boundaries between Creator and created firm. If the woman and man eat from the tree, they will be like God. The serpent equates the knowledge of good and evil with being fully divine. If they eat, they will know as much as God, and according to the serpent, God does not want that to happen. The serpent seems to play on the woman's concern about death. Her response does not indicate any desire to be like God; she simply does not want to die.

By inserting "God knows" (Gen. 3:4), the serpent continues to inject doubt. It implies that God is deliberately withholding information; it implies that God will not tolerate total equality with the human beings. The serpent does not speak again, and the woman is left to ponder what her next moves will be. As she considers the tree, we are struck by the facts omitted. She identified the tree as that in the middle of the garden in Genesis 3:3; in Genesis 3:6, she seems to be standing right next to the tree. In addition, after her conversation with the serpent, she seems to move into action. She does not draw the man into the conversation—although he seems to have been standing with her during the exchange with the serpent.

She considers the tree—it is good for food and a delight to the eyes. She is dazzled by the tree's attractive qualities. One would think that a tree of death should be ugly and disgusting; yet this tree is beautiful and alluring—thus, the temptation to resist is heightened. Perhaps both the woman and the man had been drawn to the tree from the beginning of their existence. Perhaps they discussed its pull and worked hard to resist it. Perhaps they had come close to touching or eating from the tree, only to remember the consequence before committing the act. At any rate, on this occasion, the woman makes a choice. If she would not die, why not taste? And if she would be wise for having eaten, all the better. Who would not want to be wise and knowing?

Being unselfish, the woman offers some of the fruit to the man. The text is clear: he eats it. There is no evidence in the text that the woman entices or

seduces him into eating. She does not coerce or trick him. She does not use
feminine wiles to get him to participate. What is curious is that he does not
say that she betrayed him, only that she offered and he took. He does not resist
the offer. He does not remind her of the command that he alone received. He
does not seek a way to prevent her action. He does not refuse to participate.
He is a silent, but willing, partner in the action. He is willing to push the
limits of their God-given freedom. And the results are tragic: "Then the eyes
of both were opened, and they knew that they were naked; and they sewed fig
leaves together and made loincloths for themselves" (Gen. 3:7).

This represents a major shift in their understanding of their relationship.
In Genesis 2:25, they were naked and were not ashamed. Theirs was a comfortable, harmonious, and shameless relationship. In Genesis 3:7, they seek
to cover their nakedness by making clothes. Prior to the eating of the fruit,
there was no need for clothing—they had nothing to hide. And the tension
continues to build. (Read Genesis 3:8–13.)

In this section, God addresses the man in the same manner that the serpent
addressed the woman earlier. God is once again a major character in the story.
God walks in the garden at dusk; we do not know where God has been or what
God has been doing during the day. God has to call the human beings, specifically the man. We get the sense that this is something new—God is accustomed to knowing where the human beings are; now God has to seek them.

Again, Israel portrays a God who is available. God walks in the garden and
fully interacts with the human beings. When they are not readily available,
God searches for them. God calls for the man (the pronoun "you" is singular
here). The tension continues to build—the man spills his guts! He confesses
his fear of God and his shame at being naked. Fear is a new element in the
story. In paradise, the human beings know fear and shame.

God does not deal with the issue of fear, however, but focuses on the man's
knowledge of and reaction to being naked. The man knows something that he
had not known before: fear and shame. When God asks whether the man has
eaten from the forbidden tree, he does not answer directly. In an effort to justify or protect himself, the man blames God: "The woman whom you gave to
be with me." After all, if God had not provided a helper, the man would not
have disobeyed God's direct command. Then, the man places the blame
squarely on the shoulders of the woman: "She gave me fruit from the tree,
and I ate." The man does not confess his willingness to partake of the fruit.
He does not reveal his silence in the face of the invitation to eat—he blames
God and God's created helper, the woman.

God asks the woman what she has done. She, too, does not answer
directly: "The serpent tricked me, and I ate." Her response is clear, and she
places the blame on the serpent. Unlike the man, she does not hold God

responsible for creating the serpent, and she does not incriminate her partner. She does not mention the man in her confession.

God swiftly moves to pronounce judgment. God does not question the serpent. God does not question the motives of the human beings nor does God let them explain their decision. The Divine Judge does not ask any more questions. The consequences are set forth, and all stand accused before God. Some scholars feel that the judgments describe the consequences of the actors' choices. The sentences do not represent eternal punishment for all of humankind. The serpent is cursed among all animals, is forced to crawl upon its belly (how did it move before?), and is to eat dirt. The Hebrew terminology implies that the serpent is to be the lowest of the low (even though everything was pronounced good). Further, the serpent is the enemy of the woman and her children.

The judgments on the human beings raise interesting questions. Why did the command to be fruitful and multiply not indicate whether there would be pain? Did the human beings have the freedom to reject this command to reproduce? The woman is told that she *will desire* her husband and that he will rule over her. The meaning is not clear. Most commentators lean toward the understanding that the woman will sexually desire her husband despite the consequent pain at childbirth. The second part of this pronouncement generates heated debate: "And he shall rule over you." Many take this to mean that God has cursed the woman by making her subordinate to the man. Because of the woman's disobedience, the argument goes, she is to be subservient to the man. Feminist and womanist scholars, however, suggest another understanding. This particular woman is sentenced (no explicit curse is indicated in the text) to a subordinate role to a particular man because of their mutual disobedience, not because God instituted or ordained such hierarchy. The status of the woman and the man has shifted from that of equal partners because they sinned. The text does not say that the woman is more sinful than the man; the text does not say that the woman is responsible for the fall from grace of all humanity. She and the man are sentenced to the consequences of their actions. We will revisit this thought later.

The man is also sentenced. His work of subduing the earth has become much more difficult. The man is not cursed, but the ground he works for food is. He will have to toil for a living. He will have to contend with thorns and thistles, and only by the sweat of his brow will he be able to eat. This is in contrast to his passive eating of the fruit.

All three creatures bear the consequences of their actions, but only the serpent is actually cursed. Further, the reordering of status and gender roles happens after the human beings make their choices about whether to eat the fruit. The garden had been a place of harmony, comfort, and relative freedom. Yet God has more to do: "God made garments of skins for the man and for his wife, and clothed them" (Gen. 3:21).

In the midst of divine judgment, God still is concerned about the human beings. Even though they have made loincloths from fig leaves, God clothes them in more substantial garments. God's mercy extends to them, despite their disobedience. But God has a more pressing decision to make concerning the human beings:

> Then God said, "See, the man has become like one of us, knowing good and evil; and now, he might reach out his hand and take also from the tree of life, and eat, and live forever"—therefore God sent him forth from the garden of Eden, to till the ground from which he was taken. God drove out the man; and at the east of the garden of Eden God placed the cherubim, and a sword flaming and turning to guard the way to the tree of life. (Gen. 3:22–24)

Again, God confers with the divine assembly or council. They know good and evil, and now the human beings are more like them. God is concerned that the human beings will eat from the tree of life and live forever. Remember that God did not stipulate that the tree of life was forbidden. God cannot trust the human beings any longer to obey the divine command and so casts them from the garden. They can never return; the flaming sword prevents their reentry. God seems to take a hard line here, but at the same time, God seems to continue some sense of nurture by providing substantial clothes. Nevertheless, God does not waffle on what is to happen—the human beings must go!

Whew! It has taken us a long time to get to Eve. Her story is embedded in the larger texts about creation and is mired in tradition not explicit in the text. Biblical commentators have used the texts of Genesis 1–3 to develop the concept of original sin and the fallen state of humanity. Stories about creation have been turned into religious dogma that places the blame for the ills of the world on women. Some commentators use linear logic to explain why the world is now so different from the garden. They have formulated a progressive creation: creation, paradise, and fall. Important, and all too often unanswerable, questions are evoked:

➤ What is God's role in all of this action? Initially, God is the main and only character. In the exchange between the serpent and the woman, God disappears altogether. When God reappears, it is as interrogator and judge, not as Creator and nurturer.

➤ Did God withhold important information from the human beings? If they are created in God's image and likeness, and God knows good and evil, why not the human beings, too? Was God being paternalistic by trying to protect them from this knowledge?

➤ Neither the serpent nor the human beings are characterized as evil or wicked. How, then, does Genesis 3 become the normative explanation for sin and the "fallen" state of humanity?

➤ Did God set up the human beings for failure by placing a forbidden tree in the midst of the garden?

➤ What made Eden a paradise? According to the text, the garden required human dominion and subduing. In the garden, we find loneliness, limitations, temptation, and fear. How is all this paradisiacal?

➤ Did God "use" the serpent to dupe the human beings? God created the serpent, and there is no indication that creatures other than the human beings had the freedom of choice. If the serpent was a foil, how can the woman be blamed for the fall of humankind when she simply exercised her right of choice?

Commentators call for Eve's unquestioning obedience. She should have done what God said, even though God did not speak the command to her. Because of her, according to the traditional understanding, all humankind is under the specter of sin, and it will be a long time before humanity is redeemed. The woman has been blamed, and thus all women are condemned.

A careful reading of the texts presents a different image. Eve, as the first woman, is portrayed as a character with initiative and courage. She is not the evil woman that tradition has portrayed. She is not the wicked temptress who seduces the *adam* to disobey God. She is almost childlike as she pushes against God's boundaries and tests authority. Some say she is inferior because she was created after the *adam*. In the first creation story, the creatures—human beings—formed last were considered the crown of creation. Why would that suddenly differ in the second creation story? The *adam* is considered to be the crown of God's creative work, but Eve was created last. Some say women are inferior because they were created from the *adam*'s rib, yet the *adam* was created from the dust. Neither would exist without God's breath of life.

Somehow, Eve is expected to be more obedient than the *adam*—she should have known better. The kind of trust and obedience that some would want Eve to exhibit is difficult. Mature faith and understanding come from having unsettling experiences and surviving them. In other words, we do not know we are strong until we have been tested. We do not know we believe until we have wrestled with doubts. The kind of faith that some want Eve to have can come only after she has been evicted from the garden. We want her to operate without proper information (again!). She cannot tell the difference between the serpent's words and God's word until something happens to shake up her understandings.

Faith, trust, and hope are born in the work of reordering one's chaos. In her failures Eve will learn to discern God's word. Until then, she cannot tell which words are in her best interest. She does not know whether the serpent's words are true until she tests them. And she will not be able to tell the difference as long as there are other words to be heard. God does not provide the gift of discernment before her conversation with the serpent—she has to use the resources available to her. Until she eats, how can she know that eating is wrong? Only in the aftermath does her relationship with the man and God become real; until now, she has been almost like a robot. She goes through the motions of living without understanding the depth and breadth of that living. Now she can differentiate between joy and sorrow, pleasure and pain, hope and despair. She is more fully human.

We are left to ponder a woman who is created in the image and likeness of God. The God we encounter in Genesis 1–3 talks to the void to bring forth order and beauty. This God interacts with other beings and seeks their counsel. This God appreciates symmetry and balance—day and night, sun and moon, land and water, work and rest. This God acts and makes things happen. This God is creative and appreciates the work that is done. At the same time, this God gives and withholds. This God loves and punishes. This God gives freedom and sets limits. This God welcomes and casts out.

Eve, then, has similar qualities. She thinks and speaks—with the man and the serpent and to God. She is able to engage in substantive theological debate. She respects authority and exercises her own freedoms. She appreciates beauty. She is a seeker—she wants to be better, wiser than she was created to be. The serpent does not lie to her. It states its understanding, and she makes a conscious choice. She eats because the tree is beautiful and she seeks wisdom, not because she is willful and wicked. She is an adventurous risk taker—just like God! She is courageous—she eats the fruit without knowing what the future will hold. She is willing to take the risk, despite her fear of death.

Because she has the breath of the living God within her, she can face anything. She pushes the boundaries in order to understand her freedom. She wants the freedom to truly choose. Eve's choice to eat the fruit is the first human act of independence. Her action of choice has been downgraded to sin—both the man and God seem to oppose her initiative. The man is passive and submissive before her will; yet he is quick to blame her for his choice to eat the fruit. Eve is delegated to inferior status because she considered her options, made her choice, and acted on her decision. She exercised power and became the scapegoat for humanity's sin!

In the closing verses of Genesis 3, Eve is invisible. Adam is cast out of Eden, and Eve's eviction is implied. She has been moved from a fully functioning human being with freedom of choice and strong voice to total invisibility. Eve was an intelligent and articulate being; now she is a nonentity because she tried to be all she could be.

As we consider Eve's story, we are mindful of the ways in which she has been maligned. The texts that comprise her story do not depict her as a wanton, wicked woman. She was not created to be subordinate to man. Rather, she is the active, talkative, thoughtful, adventurous one. For being so much like God, she has been blamed for all manner of troubles in the world.

By faulty extension, women today are still being blamed for the troubles of the world. Women who are smart and dare to voice their opinions are accused of being radical, aggressive, and cold. Women who are independent and adventurous are accused of undermining family values. Women are told that their place is in the home—preferably barefoot and pregnant. Our society is too "politically correct" to make this claim explicitly. So, our social and economic institutions are structured to get the message across: women still make less money than men for the same work. Women who work outside the home are still expected to manage the household chores. Women's health issues are secondary in medical research; for example, there is a cure for prostate cancer but none for breast cancer. I am not suggesting that such cures are sexist; however, if adequate resources and research were available, perhaps there would be cures for women's diseases. Male-oriented institutions continue to control women's sexuality—pro-choice and pro-life arguments are part of the public (until recently, this meant male) debate. The tenor of "family values" in some sectors of our society calls for women to leave the workplace so that men can have jobs to support their families. Women and their children are blamed for the burgeoning welfare rolls. Where are the men, and why are they not taking care of their responsibilities? Women today are encouraged to develop themselves fully, yet many continue to be held back. Women recognize that they can only go so far, that they will be stopped by a "glass ceiling." Opportunities for women are limited by the systems created by and for men.

What makes women's lives and choices so difficult is the attitude women have about themselves. Many women want to be good wives and mothers. And many want to make meaningful contributions to society. Balancing the two desires creates tension. Too often, women are forced to choose between family and work. Even in this day and age, when they have more resources and options, women agonize over their roles and status. These issues and those related to them stem from a misreading of Eve's story that extends to all women.

The texts themselves indicate that Eve was far from being inherently evil. She and the man had to live out the consequences of their actions. She was not a willful wretch; she was a woman—bold, courageous, and brilliant. We have much to learn from her!

REFLECTION QUESTIONS

1. How has the tradition about Eve shaped or influenced your perception of women in general? Has your view changed as a result of this study? Explain.
2. Male and female were created in the image and likeness of God. Why do so many people, especially women, suffer from low self-esteem?
3. In what ways are you like Eve? How are you different? This is a question for women and men!
4. When do you feel you are at your best? How do you behave during times of high self-confidence?
5. How are women being blamed for men's action or inaction today?
6. Adam blames God and the woman for his disobedience; Eve does not implicate the man. What can spouses and partners do to avoid blaming each other for the problems in their relationships?
7. Adam is passive in Genesis 1–3 and says very little. Eve is active and vocal. What are the implications of their traits for the equality and mutuality that were evident in their creation?
8. Have you ever been made to feel bad when you have voiced your opinion? What did you do?
9. What roles should women play in church and society? Be specific.
10. What is your perception of God in Genesis 1–3? What was Israel trying to say about God and the world through these stories?

2

Lot's Wife: Homicide or Suicide?

*T*he story of Lot's wife is embedded in larger stories about Abram (Abraham) and his orphaned nephew, Lot. God calls Abram out of a comfortable retirement to a new career—ancestor of a great nation yet to be formed:

> Now God said to Abram, "Go from your country and your kindred and your father's house to the land that I will show you. I will make of you a great nation, and I will bless you, and make your name great, so that you will be a blessing. I will bless those who bless you, and the one who curses you I will curse; and in you all the families of the earth shall be blessed." So Abram went, as God had told him; and Lot went with him. (Gen. 12:1–4)

It seems that Lot is a youth at the beginning of the relocation to Canaan. The caravan leaves Haran and reaches the outskirts of Canaan. God informs Abram that Canaan is the land promised to his offspring. Abram travels from Shechem to the outskirts of Bethel, toward the Negeb in the south. From his vantage point, Abram is sure that the future is bright. But there is a famine in Canaan, and Abram's caravan, including Lot, travels to Egypt, where they are alien residents. When Abram leaves Egypt and heads back toward the Negeb, Lot is still with him. By this time, Lot has acquired some wealth and is probably married. But the land is not big enough for him and Abram: "Now Lot, who went with Abram, also had flocks and herds and tents, so that the land could not support both of them living together; for their possessions were so great that they could not live together, and there was strife between the herders of Abram's livestock and the herders of Lot's livestock" (Gen. 13:5–7).

Abram proposes that they part ways, and he offers Lot his choice of location. Lot chooses the most desirable. (Read Genesis 13:10–13.) Abram's solution results in separation from his nephew. Such separations were fairly common among people of that day. However, the stage is set for disaster when we recall Genesis 12:3: "I will bless those who bless you, and the one who curses you I will curse; and in you all the families of the earth shall be blessed."

The text of Genesis 13 does not imply that Lot turns on Abram, but there is a foreshadowing of doom as a result of the separation. While they are together, both prosper. What will happen now?

Lot's choice, which seems to be the better, easier way, turns out to be trouble from the beginning: the people of Sodom are wicked and great sinners against God. Sodom was one of five cities of the Plain generally thought to surround the Dead Sea. The area was filled with sulfur and bitumen, which some commentators believe are responsible for the image of the fire-and-brimstone disaster to come. Also, the Dead Sea is the saltiest body of water on earth. It was not unusual to see salt coating rocks and trees—looking like pillars of salt.

Sodom is portrayed as a city so wicked that God had no choice but to destroy it. We do not know all of Sodom's sins, but we will get a glimpse in due time. Nothing good can happen in Sodom, and that is where Lot chooses to go.

In Genesis 14, Lot is a prisoner of war. Abram (soon to become Abraham in Genesis 17), with an army of 318 men, rescues Lot and others held captive. Abram exhibits great concern for his nephew and risks his own life in the rescue mission. In Genesis 18, Abraham and God discuss the fate of Sodom (and Gomorrah). Abraham attempts to change God's mind about the planned destruction. He asks if God plans to destroy the righteous along with the wicked. Abraham appeals to God's sense of justice: if even ten righteous people (meaning men!) can be found in Sodom, God will not destroy the city. Abraham's concern is not only for the handful of righteous people, but also for the whole city itself, even though the wicked would be saved. The few righteous have the potential of saving the wicked many. But even this reprieve will not be enough to save Sodom.

Genesis 19 is part of the J tradition. Sodom and Gomorrah are symbolic of disaster and wickedness. This chapter illustrates how disgusting the cities' inhabitants had become. Two angels enter the city of Sodom at sundown. Lot offers them an evening meal and lodging for the night. After some convincing, they agree. Before they can retire for the night, there is a commotion outside Lot's house. (Read Genesis 19:4–11.)

Lot's hospitality is challenged by the inhospitality of the mob. For those in the ancient Near East, hospitality was important—it was the act of making visitors feel at home. It meant offering them protection, and it required mutual trust between the hosts and those invited to stay at their home. Thus, Lot is in a bad situation when the mob demands the visitors. The mob's intention is to rape the strangers, and Lot's role as host is to ensure their safety. Lot is rescued from the violence of the mob after he offers his virgin daughters (!) as surrogate rape victims. The visitors blind the reckless and terrifying mob, and the Lot household avoids further danger.

The angels cannot believe the men of Sodom—the city is totally out of control. They have had it! They tell Lot to pack up and leave the city before it is destroyed: "Have you anyone else here? Sons-in-law, sons, daughters, or anyone you have in the city—bring them out of the place" (Gen. 19:12). Mrs. Lot is not mentioned.

His future sons-in-law are warned, but they laugh in Lot's face. They are determined to stay and take their chances. Likely, they are enjoying the decadence of city life. Their refusal to leave makes Lot complacent, and he follows his usual routine.

The next day, the angels again urge Lot to pack up the family and belongings and leave before disaster strikes. This time, Mrs. Lot is acknowledged: "When morning dawned, the angels urged Lot, saying, 'Get up, take your wife and your two daughters who are here, or else you will be consumed in the punishment of the city'" (Gen. 19.15).

Lot continues to dawdle; the exasperated angels finally grab Lot, Mrs. Lot, and their two daughters. The Lot family is taken out of the city and set outside the city gates (cities in the ancient Near East were surrounded by a wall for military defense purposes; gates located at various points allowed entry). The angels say to Lot (echoes of God's command to Adam): "Flee for your life; do not look back or stop anywhere in the Plain; flee to the hills, or else you will be consumed" (Gen. 19:17).

Not content to have been saved, Lot seeks to negotiate the site of his exile. Lot does not want to go to the hills as the angels recommend. He is afraid of the hills (but apparently not the destruction of Sodom and the surrounding area) and asks if he might settle in a little city near Sodom. He emphasizes the smallness of the city; perhaps he thinks small cities are less wicked than larger ones? It is clear that Lot is a city person and the hills probably present too much of a challenge for him. Remember that he also likes to take the easy way out of things. (Read Genesis 19:18–20.)

Lot's concern is clearly for himself—he does not include his wife or daughters in his plan (remember his consultation with his sons-in-law). At any rate, Lot and his family are granted asylum in Zoar. Then God begins the utter destruction and devastation of Sodom and Gomorrah, raining sulfur and fire upon them. God destroys all the cities on the Plain, the residents, and all that grew on the ground. At this point, Mrs. Lot takes center stage for a brief period. Mrs. Lot's appearances in the Bible are brief: "But Lot's wife, behind him, looked back, and she became a pillar of salt" (Gen. 19:26); and "Remember Lot's wife" (Luke 17:32).

Her story is one of the most disturbing and curious in all the Bible. She is like a ghost that haunts all who seek real answers to real questions. Because we can know so little about her, some have attempted to fill in the gaps of her story.

What can we conclude about Mrs. Lot from this account? We know that she enjoyed an urban life in the city of Sodom. She was probably thoroughly involved in the social scene—her daughters were engaged to Sodomite men. She, no doubt, enjoyed a measure of status in the city because Lot was respected and well off. It is likely that she enjoyed the perks that came with being a big fish in the big city. This is the extent of the conjectures we can make.

Commentators have tried to explain her demise by the actions of her husband, Lot. She is assumed to be a worldly, selfish woman because she was married to a man who had a bent toward the materialistic. By most accounts, Lot had done a good job of carving out a comfortable life for himself and his family. It is assumed that Mrs. Lot lived a life of ease and luxury. It is imagined that she gave exquisite dinner parties and commanded a cadre of servants. She is portrayed as a pampered and spoiled woman of means because she married well.

Biblical writers give no clues about who she is or why she came to such an abrupt end. We are simply told that she looked back and became a chunk of salt. We are left with more questions than answers about Lot's wife. We cannot be sure that she knew what was happening. When the angels told Lot to flee, Lot did not talk this over with his wife—he consulted his prospective sons-in-law. There is no evidence in the text that she heard the warning not to look back or to stop along the way. The action revolves around Lot and other men. The questions abound: What was she giving up by leaving Sodom? What could she expect in Zoar?

We know her life in Zoar would be very different from the life she enjoyed in Sodom. We do not know much about Zoar except that it was a little city. To qualify as a city, it would have to be surrounded by a wall for military protection. Also, it would have to satisfy basic needs for food and water and provide raw materials for tool making and housing. In addition, Zoar could have offered the possibility of safety from God's wrath.

All the text tells us is that Mrs. Lot became a pillar of salt. Why did she look back? As the city was being destroyed, there must have been great turmoil. There had to be people—women, children, and men—running, screaming, shouting for mercy. There must have been a tremendous outcry of pain and terror. Buildings crumbled and the earth shook. The air was filled with the pungent, choking fumes of burning sulfur. The air must have been suffocating. How could Mrs. Lot get away without looking back at the commotion and chaos? The scene must have been like a bad accident along the highway—we know we should not look, but we cannot help ourselves.

What was wrong in looking back? Today, mental health professionals encourage persons to look back—to examine their pasts for clues to destructive behaviors. These days, we challenge racial/ethnic groups to remember their history; failure to do so may result in repetition of genocide and destruction. There are periodic cultural regressions to earlier times expressed in clothing styles and music and revivals of old movies and musicals. We engage in full-scale nostalgia that harks back to a supposedly easier, less complicated time. We are a people who live in the past, trying to understand and make sense of what has happened. While we enjoy the ease that technology has provided, many of us long for the "good old days," however we define them. So, Mrs. Lot's backward glance may have been a human, instinctual move.

Was Mrs. Lot's action intentional or accidental? If she intentionally looked back, then she committed an act of suicide. As a dutiful wife, she followed her husband; for doing the right thing, she was destroyed. Did she know what awaited her in Zoar? Could she embrace the future with the same sense of confidence she had when Abram packed them up and took them on a journey whose destination was unknown? Could she trust that fitting suitors would be available to her daughters in the hill country? Could she hope that this move would be the last one? Was she simply taking one last glance at what had been her life? If she intentionally looked back, for whatever reasons, she exercised her freedom of choice.

If she knew about the command not to look back, then she took her destiny into her own hands. Perhaps she contemplated life in Zoar, the little city, and decided that the trip was not worth it. Perhaps she remembered Lot's willingness to sacrifice their innocent daughters to the violent mob just a couple of days earlier. Perhaps that act of Lot's was the straw that broke the camel's back in their marriage. As a dutiful wife, she had tried her best to support Lot. But he was not very stable. He moved around a lot, tried to take the easy path, and operated in his own best interests. Perhaps Mrs. Lot was just fed up, and death seemed like a viable option.

If she knew the command and chose to look back, she committed suicide. It was her choice regardless of what and how we might feel about such an act. For a woman with limited power, suicide might have been the desirable action.

If, however, she accidentally looked back or did not know about the prohibition, she was a victim of homicide. God murdered her! She looked back—what was wrong with that? God had agreed to save the Lot family and had taken great pains to get them out of the city before the storm of sulfur and fire. Why, then, would this woman be singled out for destruction after they had already left the wicked city of Sodom? She had not committed any known act of wickedness, so why was she turned into a pillar of salt? For this single act, she has come to symbolize all who refuse to let go of the past. Yet even the Scriptures warn the people to remember—remember how God delivered them from the hand of Pharaoh. Was Mrs. Lot not allowed to remember?

She symbolizes the defiance of all who seek the familiar and who quest for material things. Yet Lot did not fare much better—he dawdled under direct command and sniveled about the given destination. Lot was wishy-washy and halfhearted, but he and his daughters were saved and Mrs. Lot was not. Where was the justice in that? What was God doing in that instant she was frozen in place and time? Some commentators believe that Mrs. Lot was a reflection of her husband's halfheartedness and inability to act. She was destroyed because she looked back. Why was Lot not held accountable for his actions? Why was he permitted to live and not Mrs. Lot? And what did he do when she hesitated? Did he notice? Did he care? And where was God in this scenario? Where was the God of creative possibilities and second chances? Mrs. Lot seemed to have been abandoned by the God who would have saved a city for ten righteous people (men!). But Mrs. Lot did not survive—nameless and voiceless, she was gone.

This story raises uncomfortable questions. God does not look good in this story. Lot does not look good in this story. And certainly, Mrs. Lot does not look good either. It would seem that an innocent woman is sacrificed for a man who had little regard for his family. Mrs. Lot is destroyed for no good reason and God seems to abandon her. It is difficult to redeem anyone in this story. Where is the word of hope for women and men who find themselves in desperate circumstances? Where are the guidance and reassurance for women and men who must make difficult, heart-wrenching choices? Where is the presence of God for those who wrestle with overwhelming problems, situations, and conditions?

Unfortunately, Mrs. Lot is silent; we cannot learn from her directly her reasons for looking back. Perhaps some of us are like her—we do things and do not know why. We hesitate even when all seems well. We take the chance to look back when our lives lie ahead of us. We long for something other than what we have. Mrs. Lot stands as a puzzle for us, raising questions rather than providing answers. Perhaps it is enough to have the ghost of her presence to remind us that at any moment, in the twinkling of an eye, things can change. Life and death are not in our control. Mrs. Lot reminds us of the fragility of life.

REFLECTION QUESTIONS

1. What troubles you most about Mrs. Lot?
2. What purpose does her story serve in the Bible?
3. What are your perceptions of God in these passages? Think about God's relationship to Abraham, Lot, and Mrs. Lot.
4. What does her story say about marriage, then and now? If you are married, how does your spouse introduce you? Are you *"Mary,* my wife," or *"my husband, Jim"*? What does each say about the value of the person?
5. What gives your life value? Why?
6. What things should you be leaving behind? What things should you be moving toward? Be specific.
7. Is looking back wrong? Explain.
8. Answering God's call to greater service can mean giving up everything; these demands can be difficult. What happens to us when we look back?
9. Mrs. Lot was outside the city gates when she looked back. How far does one have to go to be safe? Is safety the point or aim of life? Explain.
10. Salt was an important commodity in the ancient Near East. It was used to preserve food and to purify water. It was also used for medicinal purposes. A little salt could be a lifesaver. Yet too much salt could kill human beings and vegetation. What is the significance of Mrs. Lot's transformation into a pillar of salt?

3

REBEKAH: DECEPTIVE OR DIRECT?

$\mathcal{R}$ebekah's story raises uncomfortable issues about marriage and mother-hood. Her actions were designed to assist God's plan for her family; but her methods leave much to be desired. She was Isaac's wife and mother to Esau and Jacob. Her story is embedded in the larger Abraham cycle.

Rebekah's story begins with Abraham's concern that his only son remaining at home does not marry a Canaanite woman. Abraham, in his old age, is trying to be a good father. Remember, however, that he banished his elder son, Ishmael, and the boy's mother, Hagar, because of Sarah's jealousy and resentment. You will recall that God promised that Abraham would be parent of a great nation, but Sarah, his wife, was barren. In an attempt to help God's promise to be fulfilled, Sarah provided her Egyptian servant, Hagar, as a sur-rogate mother. Any children born from Abraham and Hagar's union would legally belong to Abraham and Sarah (see Gen. 16 and 21). This arrangement sounds strange to us today; but it was the custom regarding barren wives in those days.

With the older son gone and with myriad trials, troubles, and tribulations behind him, Abraham seeks a suitable wife for Isaac. Abraham enlists the help of a trusted servant to find a wife for Isaac among Abraham's kinfolk in his country. After some discussion about his mission, the servant understands that his task is to find a willing bride for Abraham's son. The servant leaves Abraham's house with ten camels, other servants, and a treasure trove of gifts. He and his caravan reach the outskirts of Nahor and rest by a well. The servant prays that God will make clear who Isaac's future bride is to be: "Before he had finished speaking, there was Rebekah, who was born to Bethuel son of Milcah, the wife of Nahor, Abraham's brother, coming out with her water jar on her shoulder. The girl was very fair to look upon, a virgin, whom no man had known. She went down to the spring, filled her jar, and came up" (Gen. 24:15–16).

What is immediately remarkable about Rebekah is her genealogy. In most family lists, only males are named. Yet Rebekah's grandmother, Milcah, is named. We do not know a lot about Milcah: she is the daughter of Haran; she is Sarah's niece and Abraham's sister-in-law. She is Lot's sister and has eight children: "Now after these things it was told Abraham, 'Milcah also has borne children, to your brother Nahor: Uz the firstborn, Buz his brother, Kemuel the father of Aram, Chesed, Hazo, Pildash, Jidlaph, and Bethuel.' Bethuel became the father of Rebekah. These eight Milcah bore to Nahor, Abraham's brother" (Gen. 22:20–23).

It is not clear why her name is included in the genealogy, but her inclusion suggests that Rebekah strongly identifies with the matriarchs of her family.

Rebekah is characterized as a beautiful virgin who gladly does her share of work. Therefore, she will make a suitable wife for Isaac. Still, the servant is not sure she is "the one." He seeks further guidance. (Read Genesis 24:17–21.)

The servant learns more about her: she is pleasant, hospitable, kind, and considerate. The servant does one last thing to be sure that Rebekah is God's chosen mate for Isaac:

> When the camels had finished drinking, the man took a gold nose-ring weighing a half shekel, and two bracelets for her arms weighing ten gold shekels, and said, "Tell me whose daughter you are. Is there room in your father's house for us to spend the night?" She said to him, "I am the daughter of Bethuel son of Milcah, whom she bore to Nahor." She added, "We have plenty of straw and fodder and a place to spend the night." The man bowed his head and worshiped God. (Gen. 24:22–26)

When Rebekah identifies herself, she also includes her grandmother. She may be indicating the respect her grandmother garnered beyond the bearing of children; certainly, she is an important person in Rebekah's understanding of who she is. You will note that Abraham's servant asks about accommodations in Rebekah's father's house. She extends the invitation for them to stay, a prerogative generally reserved for the men of the house. She takes the responsibility to extend her family's hospitality to this stranger and his caravan. Rebekah runs straight to her mom to tell her that they are having company for the night.

At this point, Rebekah's brother, Laban, takes over and makes her invitation official. Before eating supper, the servant fills in details about his mission, and about Abraham, Sarah, and Isaac. He ends his lengthy speech with a request that Laban give Rebekah's hand in marriage to Isaac. The servant's story makes it clear that God has done the matchmaking here. But the final decision is theirs. Laban and Bethuel, Rebekah's father who has been invisible up to this point, give Rebekah away: "Then Laban and Bethuel answered, 'The thing comes from God; we cannot speak to you anything bad or good. Look, Rebekah is before you, take her and go, and let her be the wife of your master's son, as God has spoken'" (Gen. 24:50–51).

The servant worships God in thanksgiving, then presents gifts to Rebekah, her brother, and her mother. No mention is made of gifts to her father. Everyone is happy (including Rebekah?). The guests eat, drink, and sleep.

The next day, the servant is ready to return to Abraham's house with the bride-to-be. Rebekah's brother and mother (again, where is her father?) seek to delay her departure. The servant insists that they depart that day. In a remarkable show of concern, her family says the unexpected:

> "We will call the girl, and ask her." And they called Rebekah, and said to her, "Will you go with this man?" She said, "I will." So they sent away their sister Rebekah and her nurse along with Abraham's servant and his men. And they blessed Rebekah and said to her, "May you, our sister, become thousands of myriads; may your offspring gain possession of the gates of their foes." Then Rebekah and her maids rose up, mounted the camels, and followed the man; thus the servant took Rebekah, and went his way. (Gen. 24:57–61)

Although the deal has already been sealed, Rebekah has the choice of departure date. She could have stayed for ten days, and that would have been in keeping with the custom. But she chooses to leave that day. So, with her nurse and her family's blessings, Rebekah sets out to meet her husband-to-be.

She meets Isaac, and they are married. Isaac moves her into his dead mother's tent.

The focus of their wedding, however, is on Isaac, not on Rebekah who had given up her home and life to be his wife: "Then Isaac brought her into his mother Sarah's tent. He took Rebekah, and she became his wife; and he loved her. So Isaac was comforted after his mother's death" (Gen. 24:67).

The narrator does not give Rebekah's reaction or feelings. We are not told whether she loves him, only that she makes his life better since his mother's death was distressing to him. And the union of Isaac and Rebekah begins on an ominous note. Usually, a man takes his new wife into her own tent—not his mother's!

In modern terms, Rebekah and Isaac's family puts the "funk" in dysfunctional! Their family is characterized by all manner of tragedy. We know that Isaac is a mama's boy—overly attached to his mother, spoiled, and self-centered. Sarah doted on this child of her old age. But who can blame Isaac for his character? His father tried to sacrifice him (Gen. 22). He watched his father expel his older brother and stepmother into the wilderness (Gen. 21). He witnessed his mother's anger, jealousy, and resentment toward Hagar and Ishmael. He had heard the story of how his father pretended that Sarah was his sister to save his own hide. His own father almost forced his mother into adultery because he was afraid to be honest about being her husband (Gen. 12 and 20). Isaac grew up in a dysfunctional family filled with tension, deception, and violence. This all seemed normal to him. His hopes for a happy and healthy family are doomed from the start. The account of Isaac's childhood may seem overblown as we look back on it. However, the point is that Isaac brought unresolved issues to his marriage to Rebekah.

Further, he and Rebekah are married for twenty years, and still there is no child. For Isaac, this must seem like déjà vu all over again—his own mother was barren. She did not have Isaac until well past her childbearing years. Through much prayer, Rebekah conceives: "Isaac prayed to God for his wife, because she was barren; and God granted his prayer, and his wife Rebekah conceived" (Gen. 25:21).

Another remarkable aspect of Rebekah's story is that we have some sense of her inner life. Her pregnancy is hard, and she prays for understanding. God speaks directly to her:

> The children struggled together within her; and she said, "If it is to be this way, why do I live?" So she went to inquire of God. And God said to her,

> "Two nations are in your womb,
> and two peoples born of you shall be divided;
> the one shall be stronger than the other,
> the elder shall serve the younger."

> When her time to give birth was at hand, there were twins in her womb. The first came out red, all his body like a hairy mantle; so they named him Esau. Afterward his brother came out, with his hand gripping Esau's heel; so he was named Jacob. Isaac was sixty years old when she bore them. (Gen. 25:22–26)

The stage is set for more dysfunction: sibling rivalry will tear the family apart; and the law of the elder brother inheriting the father's estate will be compromised—more ominous notes. The boys fight while still in Rebekah's womb. During the birth, Jacob reaches out of the birth canal and grabs his brother's heel. We get the impression that these two will not be getting along with each other!

There is no indication in the text that Rebekah shares God's pronouncement about their sons with Isaac. To make matters worse, each parent is guilty of blatant favoritism: "Isaac loved Esau, because he was fond of game; but Rebekah loved Jacob" (Gen. 25:28).

Nothing good can come of this situation. The writer does not implicate God in this affair beyond the divine pronouncement. Things will turn out tragically because of the persons involved. The theological task is to determine what God does with this mess.

The twins are starkly different from each other: Esau is ruddy, hairy, and most comfortable hunting in the woods. Jacob, on the other hand, is mild-mannered, smooth-skinned, and a homebody. The tension grows. One day Esau comes home from a hard day of hunting, and he is hungry and tired. He asks Jacob, who is cooking, for some stew. Jacob agrees—only if Esau sells his birthright, which he does.

The issue of birthright does not mean much to us, but the issue was a big deal in ancient Israel. The birthright is the oldest son's inheritance, usually a double portion. The eldest son assumes the leadership of the family when the father dies. To lose his birthright is to lose his claim on his father's estate. In this story, the brothers relate differently to the issue of birthright. Esau appears rather foolish for giving up his future security and status for a bowl of stew. Jacob seems ready to take unfair advantage of his older brother's weakness. It is difficult to see who is more at fault here. Both make decisions out of their self-interest: Esau's concern is for the immediate present; Jacob's concern is for the near future. Both fail to honor family values and relationships. Things can only get worse.

Isaac is aging and finds himself facing challenges: there is a famine in the land, and he and his family become alien residents (remember Abraham and Lot?) in Gerar, a city belonging to the Philistines. When the men of Gerar ask about Rebekah, Isaac lies and says she is his sister (this is more than déjà vu all over again; his father did the same thing with Sarah when they were residents in Egypt although, technically, Sarah was Abraham's half sister; see Gen. 20:1–13). The motivation is the same—each man lies to save his own hide and is willing to sacrifice his wife in the process. Isaac's deception is discovered before any harm is done.

Isaac prospers in Gerar and finds himself in conflict with the men of the city over wells and water rights. After several moves, Isaac makes a pact with the king. Isaac and his family peacefully settle in Beer-sheba.

The family strife continues. Remember how firm Abraham was about Isaac's not marrying a Canaanite woman? Guess what Esau does? Yes—he marries two Hittite (Canaanite) women, Judith and Basemath, who make life miserable for Isaac and Rebekah (Gen. 26:35). This act of defiance only fore-shadows the tragedy related in Genesis 27–28. Rebekah eavesdrops on a conversation between Isaac and his favorite son, Esau. Isaac knows that his death is imminent. He wants to share a last meal with Esau, and at their last supper, Isaac will bless him. Rebekah, perhaps remembering the pronouncement concerning the elevation of the younger son, conspires with Jacob to have Isaac's blessing bestowed upon her favorite son:

Rebekah said to her son Jacob, "I heard your father say to your brother Esau, 'Bring me game, and prepare for me savory food to eat, that I may bless you before God before I die.' Now therefore, my son, obey my word as I command you. Go to the flock, and get me two choice kids, so that I may prepare from them savory food for your father, such as he likes; and you shall take it to your father to eat, so that he may bless you before he dies.'" (Gen. 27:6–10)

Rebekah has a clear plan in mind; she knows how to implement the plan, too. But she needs Jacob's cooperation to pull it off:

But Jacob said to his mother Rebekah, "Look, my brother Esau is a hairy man, and I am a man of smooth skin. Perhaps my father will feel me, and I shall seem to be mocking him, and bring a curse on myself and not a blessing." His mother said to him, "Let your curse be on me, my son; only obey my word, and go, get them for me." (Gen. 27:11–13)

Jacob's hesitation stems from fear of being caught and cursed by his father. There is no indication that he objects for moral or religious reasons. He is willing to go along with his mother's plot if his safety is guaranteed. He has already stolen his brother's birthright; he has no problem stealing his blessing.

Rebekah volunteers to assume the curse if the plan fails. She is totally dedicated to making Jacob the legally favored son. She orders him to do as she says, and he complies. (Read Genesis 27:14–17.)

Jacob implements the plan without flaw. Although Isaac seems suspicious, he is finally convinced that his son Esau is with him and confers the blessing upon Jacob. Jacob has barely left his father's room when Esau enters. When he learns that Jacob has cheated him of his father's final blessing, he goes ballistic! "When Esau heard his father's words, he cried out with an exceedingly great and bitter cry, and said to his father, 'Bless me, me also, father!'" (Gen. 27:34).

Esau begs for a blessing for himself and receives a blessing of sorts: his life will be in an infertile, dry land, and his days will be marked by violence and hatred for his brother. Esau's feelings toward Jacob have already turned to hatred. Esau is bitter because Jacob has stolen his birthright and his blessing. For all practical purposes, Jacob has usurped his brother's position as elder son. Esau decides to kill Jacob when Isaac dies. Rebekah is privy to this information, but we are not told how she finds out his plan. (Read Genesis 27:41–42.)

Rebekah devises a plan to protect her precious Jacob from murder: "Now therefore, my son, obey my voice; flee at once to my brother Laban in Haran, and stay with him a while, until your brother's fury turns away—until your brother's anger against you turns away, and he forgets what you have done to him; then I will send, and bring you back from there. Why should I lose both of you in one day?" (Gen. 27:43–45).

Her plan is to simply send Jacob away until Esau cools down. She sends Jacob to her home and her brother, Laban. She is hoping to send for Jacob after a time. She is concerned for Esau, too. If Esau kills Jacob, he will be executed, and she will have lost both sons.

In a rare moment of intimacy with Isaac, Rebekah expresses concern that Jacob will marry a Hittite woman and her life will not be worth living if he does. Isaac takes action by calling Jacob. He warns him about marrying a Canaanite woman and, with a blessing, sends him off to Laban. So, it appears that Jacob's departure is Isaac's idea. Isaac does not know that Esau is planning to kill his younger brother. Isaac thinks he is merely sending Jacob away to find an Israelite bride. There is no evidence in the text that Isaac knows of Esau's plot.

Esau, however, witnesses Jacob's departure and knows that his parents do not want him to marry a Canaanite woman. Esau acts out again by marrying Ishmael's daughter. Remember that Ishmael is Isaac's older brother. Esau marries within the family, but within the outcast part of it.

This is the last we hear of Rebekah until we learn of her burial site in Genesis 49:31. Rebekah is cast as a deceiving, lying woman who stops at nothing to see her favorite son get the benefits reserved for the elder son. Yet she is the active player in this family. She speaks, prays, develops, and implements courses of action, and she is willing to deal with consequences. Rebekah's life is characterized by a level of freedom we have not seen in other women's lives at this point. It is true that her freedom is limited within the patriarchy; however, we see more of her life than of many other women in the Bible. She understands her role in the culture of her day, but pushes the boundaries. She dutifully goes about her chores, makes her trips to the well, and extends hospitality to strangers. She identifies herself through her father *and* her grandmother. She is sure of herself as she engages in a conversation with Abraham's servant, a stranger to her. She shows great courage and self-assurance when she packs up her belongings and journeys to a strange land to marry Isaac, another stranger. She shows a life of faith and prayer when she inquires of God about her pregnancy. She shows great curiosity about the warring between her sons while they were still enclosed in her body. She shows ingenuity in devising her plan to ensure God's pronouncement about Jacob. While we might quibble with her tactics, we cannot criticize her motives. She really believes she is doing God's work and will. She is the major player in Isaac's story. All that she does, she does for her son, God's chosen and favored one.

She could have done some things differently. She could have communicated better with her husband. She could have worked to ensure a healthier relationship between her sons. She could have created an atmosphere where Isaac could have interacted with both of his sons. While we cannot condone her manipulation of Isaac, we can try to understand her actions. Aside from her theological motivation, Rebekah may have harbored some real hurts of her own. She left her family to marry a man she had never known. On their honeymoon, Isaac took her to his mother's tent rather than to one he prepared for her. We do not know how Rebekah felt about or reacted to this situation. Isaac was willing to sacrifice her person and sexuality to save himself from possible death. Yet we are told that he loved her! What kind of love treats a beloved in that way?

Rebekah gives up her life to be Isaac's wife, and then she is childless for twenty years. She seems destined for shame and poverty following Isaac's death. When she does become pregnant, it is a violent, unpleasant experience. She marries into a dysfunctional family, and the cycle continues in her own. Her freedom is exercised in the private sphere of family and home. Yet in the midst of such challenges, Rebekah proves to be a strong woman—she takes matters into her own hands and works her plan to perfection. She is brave, courageous, and bold. She has an active prayer life, at least at various points in her life. Unfortunately, she pays a price for her freedom. She never sees her beloved Jacob after she sends him away. She does not see him claim his birthright and blessing. She never sees or nurtures her grandchildren. Because they never meet her, she never knows whether her grandchildren claim her in their self-identification. She does not have her favorite son to comfort her in her old age and dying days. Rebekah may have thought she was doing God's work. But she betrayed her husband and her oldest son. Rebekah is a reflection of many women who love unwisely; her love for Jacob made her hurt the other men in her life.

If we are able to see beyond the hurt Rebekah causes her family and herself, we see a woman with remarkable skills. She is intellectually gifted and able to see a bigger picture. She is a logical thinker and understands cause and effect. She is willing to take chances and thinks well on her feet. She is willing to sacrifice her own comfort for the sake of her favorite child. Rebekah is a woman who always tries to do the right thing. We are left to wonder what would have happened if she had not taken matters into her own hands.

Rebekah was a woman whose drive and creativity were stifled by the patriarchal norms of her day. In another place and time, she might have been a major leader in politics or industry. But she used her power within the limits of her status; she was a mover and shaker motivated by a deep sense of faith and destiny. Rebekah was a reflection of women, especially mothers, the world over who seek the highest good for their children. Beyond being a mother, she was a woman in her own right. Her self-identification with her grandmother gave us a glimpse of what she might have become had she been really and truly free.

ℛEFLECTION QUESTIONS

1. Rebekah has a deep, sincere prayer life. How do you describe your prayer life?
2. Rebekah lists her grandmother in her self-identification. What would happen if you thought of yourself in terms of the women in your family? Would this make a difference in how you see yourself?
3. Rebekah uses questionable means to achieve divine ends. In this way, she mirrors Sarah. Do you believe that ends justify means? Explain.
4. If you are married or in a committed relationship, do you keep secrets from your spouse or partner? Why? What are the consequences, if any, of total honesty? Is it possible to be totally honest in relationships?
5. What are Rebekah's strengths and weaknesses? How do they compare to your own?
6. Rebekah was forced to live in the house with men she had betrayed. How do you think she handled this? How would you handle a similar situation?
7. Do you think Rebekah had women friends? What do you imagine they talked about?

4

TAMAR: PARASITE OR PERSISTENT?

There are three women named Tamar in the Hebrew Scriptures: Judah's daughter-in-law, Absalom's sister, and Absalom's only daughter. Our focus is on Tamar, Judah's daughter-in-law. Her story is one of extraordinary courage and resoluteness. She goes to great lengths and considerable risk to achieve her goal of bearing children. She overshadows Judah, who is the other major character in the story. Be warned! This is an X-rated story filled with sexual intrigue and espionage.

Judah is the fourth son born to Jacob and Leah. We have already seen how Jacob's family displayed unhealthy tendencies; we will see that the dysfunction continues. This family story is generally assigned to the J tradition and highlights some basic human concerns: parental anguish and love, duty and honor, guilt and righteousness, trickery and revelation, childlessness and sibling rivalry.

Judah leaves his family and settles in a town not far from Bethlehem. There, he marries a Canaanite woman who is never named. She bears three sons for Judah: Er, Onan, and Shelah. Judah chooses a wife for his eldest son; her name is Tamar. We do not know much about Tamar. She was probably a Canaanite woman, but we have no sense of her ancestry—no genealogy is given for her. Her identity contrasts sharply with that of Rebekah who self-identifies with men and women in her family; Tamar simply appears without a past.

Er, Judah's eldest son, is a wicked man. The text does not say in what ways he is wicked, so we do not know what he has done that would result in death. We are told that because of his wickedness, he was put to death by God.

The next son was obligated, according to the law of the Israelites, to marry his brother's widow. Any children resulting from this union would legally belong to the deceased brother:

> When brothers reside together, and one of them dies and has no son, the wife of the deceased shall not be married outside the family to a stranger. Her husband's brother shall go in to her, taking her in marriage, and performing the duty of a husband's brother to her, and the firstborn whom she bears shall succeed to the name of the deceased brother, so that his name may not be blotted

out of Israel. But if the man has no desire to marry his brother's widow, then his brother's widow shall go up to the elders at the gate and say, "My husband's brother refuses to perpetuate his brother's name in Israel; he will not perform the duty of a husband's brother to me." Then the elders of his town shall summon him and speak to him. If he persists, saying, "I have no desire to marry her," then his brother's wife shall go up to him in the presence of the elders, pull his sandal off his foot, spit in his face, and declare, "This is what is done to the man who does not build up his brother's house." Throughout Israel his family shall be known as "the house of him whose sandal was pulled off." (Deut. 25:5–10)

The *levir* (duty of a husband's brother) is called the levirate law and was instituted to protect the husband's bloodline; there was not much concern for the woman in this situation. However, she would be provided for through her sons. Failure to honor the conditions of the levirate custom resulted in family shame.

Onan is ordered to marry Tamar, to perform the duty of a surrogate husband, and to raise his dead brother's child. For reasons that we are not told, Onan resists following the custom. To avoid bringing shame on his family, he has sex with Tamar on a regular basis, but he practices a form of birth control by spilling "his semen on the ground" (Gen. 38:9). He has fulfilled the duty of a brother-in-law but preempts the possibility of impregnating her. He has done his part, so it is not his "fault" if Tamar does not conceive, or at least, that seems to be his rationale. Some commentators speculate that Onan did not fully comply with the levirate custom because he was not willing to give up his chance of getting Er's inheritance for himself. His attempt at deception is displeasing to God, and he, too, is put to death.

Poor Tamar, twice a widow and no children! Tamar finds herself in a bad situation. She has no man or child to give her life meaning and status in the patriarchal society in which she lives. Her last hope is that Shelah will make her an "honest woman."

But Judah short-circuits the matter; he tells Tamar to go back to her father's house until Shelah grows up. His concern is not for Shelah's age. Rather, he wants to keep his son alive. He assumes that the demise of his two sons is Tamar's fault. There must be something wrong with her because her husbands keep dying. It seems never to occur to Judah that his sons are responsible for their own deaths.

At any rate, Tamar is pushed out of Judah's home and sent back to her folks. Such action is irregular in that era and pushes Tamar even closer to the margins. As a childless widow in her father's house, she is in danger—she has no future financial security because she is cut off from her husband's family and inheritance. Moreover, she is not legally free to marry anyone else as long as a brother of her husband is alive. She is an outcast in both Judah's house and her father's house. She, no doubt, frets about her future and tries to be patient with the arrangement.

After an appropriate amount of time has passed, Tamar realizes that Judah has no intention of making Shelah available to her. In all likelihood, she thinks long and hard about the course of action she should take to hold him legally accountable. In her day, women were not encouraged to be straightforward and aggressive, so she could not confront Judah directly about his lack of honor. She would have to come up with something much more subtle.

It is not long before the perfect opportunity presents itself:

> In course of time the wife of Judah, Shua's daughter, died; when Judah's time of mourning was over, he went up to Timnah to his sheepshearers, he and his friend Hirah the Adullamite. When Tamar was told, "Your father-in-law is going up to Timnah to shear his sheep," she put off her widow's garments, put on a veil, wrapped herself up, and sat down at the entrance to Enaim, which is on the road to Timnah. She saw that Shelah was grown up, yet she had not been given to him in marriage. When Judah saw her, he thought her to be a prostitute, for she had covered her face. He went over to her at the road side, and said, "Come, let me come in to you," for he did not know that she was his daughter-in-law. She said, "What will you give me, that you may come in to me?" He answered, "I will send you a kid from the flock." And she said, "Only if you give me a pledge, until you send it." He said, "What pledge shall I give you?" She replied, "Your signet and your cord, and the staff that is in your hand." So he gave them to her, and went in to her, and she conceived by him. Then she got up and went away, and taking off her veil she put on the garments of her widowhood. (Gen. 38:12–19)

Tamar knows the widower will be amenable to sexual activity, and she uses the power of her sexuality to achieve her ends. She places herself in his way; Judah assumes she is a prostitute and negotiates the terms of their sexual tryst. Tamar is quite shrewd in her dealings with Judah. She does not simply take his word that he will provide the payment of a young goat. After all, he has lied about giving her to Shelah in marriage; why should she believe him now? She requires a pledge or collateral before she consents to sex with him. He willingly gives his signet, cord, and staff. That he would so easily hand over his means of identification and objects of his status seems risky. The signet is his official means of identifying himself. The signet is used as a seal (or mark) and confers legal consent. His cord holds the signet around his neck. His staff controls his flock and is a symbol of authority. Further, his staff protects him from robbers or wild animals. These items seem to be a lot of collateral, but he gives them to her.

Judah and Tamar have sex, and she becomes pregnant. Judah never recognizes her; for him, Tamar has become a nonperson. She is an object for Judah's sexual desire and nothing more. After her encounter with Judah, Tamar puts her widow's garb back on and returns to her father's house.

Judah sends his friend to give the "prostitute" the goat and to retrieve Judah's collateral. The friend asks the townspeople about the "temple prostitute." Judah's friend uses this term that designates an aspect of Canaanite religion. Prostitutes made themselves available as part of a fertility rite to which Israel was strongly opposed. There is little evidence that this practice actually took place; but there are references to it throughout the Hebrew Scriptures.

The townspeople tell him there has been no prostitute in the area. The friend goes back to Judah and reports his findings. Judah dismisses the matter, even though his identity is at stake. He has no legal way to prove who he is. His identity is in Tamar's possession. She literally has him! Judah feels justified in that he tried to keep his end of the bargain, but he desires to save face and lets the woman keep his things. He does not want to admit that he has been fooled by a prostitute.

Great tension is in this episode, and we are anxious to find out what happens next. The writer has created a strong level of suspense and anxiety. We are not kept waiting:

> About three months later Judah was told, "Your daughter-in-law Tamar has played the whore; moreover she is pregnant as a result of whoredom." And Judah said, "Bring her out, and let her be burned." As she was being brought out, she sent word to her father-in-law, "It was the owner of these who made me pregnant." And she said, "Take note, please, whose these are, the signet and the cord and the staff." Then Judah acknowledged them and said, "She is more in the right than I, since I did not give her to my son Shelah." And he did not lie with her again. (Gen. 38:24–26)

This part of the story is unsettling. The power of patriarchy is shown at its worst. Judah attempts to exercise the prerogative of the male head of the family who has been dishonored by the sexual activity of the woman. Tamar is in danger.

When word gets out that Tamar is pregnant, she is accused of being a whore. Because she is a widow, her act and resulting pregnancy would be considered an act of adultery. According to Israelite law, both partners of the adultery should be killed: "If a man commits adultery with the wife of his neighbor, both the adulterer and the adulteress shall be put to death" (Lev. 20:10).

Judah's duty, representing the wronged husband, would be to find the man and have both the man and Tamar stoned. However, Judah immediately judges, convicts, and condemns Tamar. Her "punishment" is extreme—stoning would not be enough. He wants her and her unborn child burned and reduced to ashes. He wants to utterly destroy a woman he has blamed for the deaths of his sons and has already cast out of his household. As the head of the family, he has the right to determine her fate. How ironic it would be if he discovers that she "transgressed" with the father of her husband: "If a man lies with his daughter-in-law, both of them shall be put to death; they have committed perversion, their blood is upon them" (Lev. 20:12); and "You shall not uncover the nakedness of your daughter-in-law: she is your son's wife; you shall not uncover her nakedness" (Lev. 18:15).

Although Judah does not recognize Tamar as his daughter-in-law when they have their sexual encounter, he is guilty of committing a crime punishable by death. The tension mounts. Tamar sends the symbols that identify the man who made her pregnant—and Judah knows he is the man!

According to custom, both should have been killed. But Judah commutes her death sentence and gives her due respect. To do any less would result in his own demise. He acknowledges the righteousness of her action and *lets* her live. To kill her would mean suicide for him, for he, too, is a guilty party. Tamar's act places Judah, herself, and their child in jeopardy. Had the act been made public, all three would have been killed. Imagine Judah's reaction when the messenger presented his very own signet, cord, and staff! This woman—an outcast with no means of support, banished to her father's house—has proven to be a worthy opponent. She has figured out a way to make Judah accountable to the justice that is her due.

It is important to understand the gravity of Tamar's strategy. She fits the characterization of the biblical trickster (see p. 20 of Susan Niditch reference, found in Newsom and Ringe in the Resources section). A trickster, in this sense, is one who is able to change the course of events by taking definitive action. A trickster is shrewd, insightful, creative; a trickster is not a clown or silly person. A trickster is one who uses whatever power is available to change the course of action. Along these lines, the serpent in the Eve story is a trickster. Rebekah is a trickster when she plots to make Jacob the favored son. Tamar fits the definition perfectly. Given the reality of patriarchy, she is expected to accept her fate on the margins of society and live off the kindness of strangers.

She sees other possibilities, however, and goes to great lengths to secure her future. She counts the risk and forges ahead. She has nothing to lose because she has nothing—no family protection, no viable means of support, no offspring to help her. She pushes the edges of tradition and wins. Again, the end justifies the extreme means. Her actions show her to be a daring risk taker for the sake of the future. Even more amazing is the fact that she wins, and she is a Canaanite woman. This combination is usually destroyed in Israel.

The end of her story would seem to indicate that the family drama of dysfunction will continue. (Read Genesis 38:27–30.) Like Rebekah, Judah's grandmother, she gives birth to twins. The twins are in conflict, as were Judah's father and his uncle, Esau. Her son, Perez, carries the family name for David and Jesus. Tamar remains the major player in this story—and stories yet to be revealed.

Tamar was a woman of striking resourcefulness within limited circumstances and conditions. She used what she had—sexual power and ingenuity—to get what she wanted—financial security and status as a mother. She made Judah recognize her personhood and held him accountable to provide the justice she deserved. She did that at great risk to both of them. He acknowledged that she was "in the right," a description rarely used of women and even more rarely in relation to Canaanite women. She fought the law, and this time, she won.

Tamar is reflective of women throughout history who have had to resort to using their bodies in order to survive. I imagine that Tamar would have preferred another means to achieve the security she sought. The court system, however, would not have heard her case. She would have been accused of a frivolous lawsuit. Her charge of neglect would have been thrown out because there was insufficient evidence. Today, she might have to go on welfare for a time, and her assistance would be meager because she had no children. While Tamar is resourceful and adventurous, she may need a period of time to implement a plan for survival.

Tamar embodies women who are victimized by systems. She has the law on her side, but only extraordinary proof makes it possible for her to win. Many women get lost in the red tape of bureaucracy. They use the means at their disposal and too often these resources are not enough.

Who knows if Tamar would be homeless, helpless, hopeless? Her situation is too often duplicated throughout the world where women suffer undue hardship for no reason other than being born female. Tamar's plight is all too familiar and haunts us today. That she dared to do something about her situation is an inspiration. Yet for all her risk taking, we are not sure whether she really triumphed. Judah did not acknowledge her as his wife, and we can only assume that he provided basic child support. She had no way of making him pay for the wrong he did to her. So, in the end, she got what she needed, but maybe not what she wanted.

REFLECTION QUESTIONS

1. Tamar uses her "feminine wiles" to achieve financial security. How do women use the power of their sexuality and their bodies today?

2. Judah clearly violated the law by withholding Shelah from Tamar. Was she justified by implementing her plan to hold Judah legally accountable for her well-being? Explain.

3. Tamar shows great savvy in her negotiations with Judah at the roadside of Enaim. How did she know the art of the deal? What character traits does Tamar exhibit in the exchange at the roadside?

4. Judah had relegated Tamar to nonperson status when he banished her to her father's house. Have you ever felt like a nonperson? How did you regain your sense of self?

5. Patriarchy claims control of women's sexuality for the purposes of perpetuating men's family lines. In what ways do we still live under patriarchal assumptions about women's sexuality—consider the issues of birth control, abortion, and women's health care issues.

6. How might men behave to truly honor and respect women?

7. A feature of being a "bad girl" is the necessity of deceit. In other words, sometimes women have to be naughty in order to be noticed. How does this apply to Tamar? How does it apply to you?

8. Should Judah have been punished for jeopardizing Tamar's future? Explain. What would be a fitting punishment?

9. Tamar's childlessness did not result from barrenness. The fault was with her husbands. How did this reality prompt Tamar to take matters into her own hands?

10. Judah blames Tamar for the deaths of his sons. How are women still being blamed for men's disasters?

11. The text states that Judah never had sex with Tamar after the roadside incident. We can assume that Judah did not marry her, but provided financial support. How does her situation reflect modern circumstances for women?

12. Tamar took great risk to have a child. Compare her drive to that of some young women and girls today who long to have children to supply the love missing in their lives. What are some reasons women want to have children?

13. There is a tendency in our culture to blame the mother for the ills and dysfunction of adult children. What might Tamar's sons say about her?

14. Judah sends Tamar to her father's house as a way of getting rid of her. She is a stranger in both Judah's house and her father's house. She does not have a place to belong. Have you ever felt like an outsider? How did you handle the situation?

15. What advice would you give to Tamar if she asked you? Be specific.

5

POTIPHAR'S WIFE: TRUTH OR DARE?

$\mathcal{T}$he story of Potiphar's wife is an episode in the larger Joseph story. Her presence is essential to his development and leadership. She plays an essential role, by extension, in the salvation history of Israel.

Joseph is the elder son born to Jacob (Rebekah's son!) and Rachel. He is Jacob's favorite son, although Joseph is not the firstborn son. (Déjà vu all over again. Remember that Esau was his father's favorite and Jacob was his mom's.) Given his history, you would think that Jacob would have learned something about family life. In Genesis 37, we have a mixed picture of Joseph—he works cooperatively with his brothers, but tends to give his father bad reports about them. We are warned of impending tragedy early in the story: "Now Israel [Jacob] loved Joseph more than any other of his children, because he was the son of his old age; and he had made him a long robe with sleeves. But when his brothers saw that their father loved him more than all his brothers, they hated him, and could not speak peaceably to him" (Gen. 37:3–4).

Sibling hostility against Joseph is generated by Jacob's obvious love for him. The other sons hate Joseph and do not direct their anger and resentment toward their father. The father's love is embodied and expressed in a long robe with sleeves, a visible sign of Jacob's high regard for this child of his old age and his favorite wife.

Through his interpretation of two dreams, Joseph claims that he will rule over his family. His claim makes his brothers despise him even more. The stage is set for tragic events because there is great tension in the family. The brothers, without Joseph, take Jacob's flock from Hebron to a place near Shechem. Jacob sends Joseph to find his brothers, and he is to report back to Jacob. Joseph is not able to locate them at first because they have moved on to Dothan. When they see Joseph approaching in his fancy robe, they plot to kill him. They feel that killing the dreamer will prevent the dream's fulfillment. Only Reuben utters a word of reason: he suggests that they not kill him. Reuben's plan is to have Joseph thrown into a pit until Reuben can privately rescue him. The others agree to cast Joseph into a pit.

They snatch Joseph, take his robe, and throw him into an empty, waterless pit. While the brothers are eating supper, they see a caravan of Ishmaelites (remember Isaac's half brother, Hagar's son?) on its way to Egypt. Judah has the bright idea to sell Joseph to the Ishmaelites; that way, they will not be guilty of murder. The brothers agree. Joseph is sold for twenty pieces of silver and taken to Egypt. There he is sold to Potiphar, an official of Pharaoh's court.

Apparently, Reuben had gone off to tend the flock because he returns to the pit to find Joseph gone. He is so distressed that the other brothers devise a plan to cover up their deed. They take Joseph's robe, dip it in goat's blood, and present it to Jacob as proof of Joseph's untimely demise.

Jacob is extremely distraught, mourns for many days, and cannot be comforted. (Remember that Jacob deceived his father just as his sons are deceiving him!) The tension of the story increases because we are left to wonder whether Joseph's dreams of leadership will be fulfilled.

The narrator tells us that Joseph does very well in Potiphar's household because God is with him. In fact, Potiphar promotes Joseph to head of the household. Because of Joseph, Potiphar also prospers, and Potiphar thoroughly trusts Joseph. All of this seems too good to be true. Sadly, it is—enter Mrs. Potiphar.

Mrs. Potiphar is every man's nightmare—the woman who cries rape when none occurred. Commentators generally agree that the story of Potiphar's wife resembles other tales prevalent in the ancient Near East. The biblical rendition is similar to the Egyptian version called "Tale of Two Brothers" as well as the Gilgamesh epic (see p. 24 of Susan Niditch reference, found in Newsom and Ringe in the Resources section). The theme is simple: the evil female character plays a positive role concerning the hero and his culture. The plot is predictable: a woman makes vain attempts to seduce a good man who resists. He is falsely accused of trying to force her. The good man is punished for his alleged attempt at rape. The woman says nothing in his defense, and she disappears from the story. The folktale emphasizes the physical qualities of the man, who is usually quite handsome and manly. The woman is usually older and has a measure of power or authority over the man. Her accusation is not questioned, and punishment is meted out by another man who is powerful enough to enforce the punishment. The young man is removed from the center of the story. Sometimes, the hero is killed and returns from the dead. The story of Mrs. Potiphar includes these elements. (Read Genesis 39:6–20.)

Usual discussions of this text focus on the negative actions of Mrs. Potiphar toward Joseph. She is portrayed as a foreign temptress who threatens to jeopardize God's will for Joseph. A closer look, however, reveals interesting aspects of her story.

Potiphar has complete faith and trust in Joseph. The text indicates that Joseph is "handsome and good-looking." Without a doubt, he is a hunk! No doubt he causes quite a stir among the women in the household as he goes about his duties. We know he has a penchant for colorful, flamboyant clothes. (Remember the robe his father gave him? His brothers could see him in it from far off. Joseph wore his robe everywhere, including into the fields to check on his brothers.) It is likely that he continued to sport fashionable clothes. That he is successful and prosperous affirms this possibility.

Mrs. Potiphar is never named, but her elevated status is made clear—she is Joseph's master's wife. As woman of the house, she owes Joseph no special respect and states her desires directly: "Lie with me!" Joseph refuses, based on his loyalties to Potiphar and to God. Potiphar has given him equal authority within the household; the only thing not under his control and authority is Mrs. Potiphar. Joseph seems appalled that she would even think he would be a willing partner in her potential adulterous act. Further, he sees adultery as a sin against God. He tries to appeal to her political and religious sensibilities. In the process, Joseph comes off looking pretty good—a conscientious, loyal, devout worker.

Mrs. Potiphar refuses to take no for an answer and repeats her demand day after day. Perhaps she thinks persistence will win him over. Perhaps she thinks he will give in to her desires so she will leave him alone. However, Joseph does not relent. We are not told how she reacts to his refusals. As a woman married to a man of great wealth and status, Mrs. Potiphar is accustomed to having her way. That this silly young man, with his platitudes about loyalty to God and Potiphar, would dare refuse her is unconscionable.

She continues her demands. One day, when no one else is in the house, she grabs his garment (remember when his brothers took his robe just before throwing him into a pit?) and repeats her desire, "Lie with me!" Joseph does the honorable thing at the time—he leaves his garment and flees the scene. She sees her chance to show him who is really in control. She calls out to the other members of the household and tells the lie. She exaggerates the seriousness of the event. Joseph is a Hebrew, a foreigner, and she plays on the xenophobic suspicions of the Egyptians. His attempted rape of her is an insult to the entire household because it shows a lack of respect and honor. And she has proof—his garment, which he leaves in his haste to flee the scene. There are no witnesses; it is her word against his. Further, she blames the entire sordid mess on her husband, who had the poor judgment to bring Joseph into their household. (Remember when Adam blamed God for providing Eve as a helper?)

When Potiphar gets home, he has to decide how to handle the situation. He feels guilty that he has brought shame into his home by hiring Joseph. Potiphar is dutifully and predictably outraged by this turn of events. He does not question his wife, Joseph, or the other members of the household. He assumes the worst is true and has Joseph imprisoned.

Mrs. Potiphar disappears from history at this point. She is left as a villain. And Joseph, although falsely imprisoned, continues:

> God was with Joseph and showed him steadfast love; God gave him favor in the sight of the chief jailer. The chief jailer committed to Joseph's care all the prisoners who were in the prison, and whatever was done there, he was the one who did it. The chief jailer paid no heed to anything that was in Joseph's care, because God was with him; and whatever he did, God made it prosper. (Gen. 39:21–23)

Joseph is an innocent victim for whom God continues to care. Even as an inmate, Joseph prospers; he impresses the warden, who gives him more and more responsibility. Eventually, Joseph will be released from prison and elevated to a position higher than that he held in Potiphar's house. His dream of being a man of great power and wealth will come to pass.

Though a villain, Potiphar's wife has played a major and essential role in moving Israel's history along. Joseph emerges as a hero who beats all odds. His trials, troubles, and tribulations make him stronger. God takes the stuff of his life and turns it into opportunities.

Mrs. Potiphar is most often portrayed in a negative light—she demands, seduces, and lies. She is almost a caricature of the sexually powerful and evil woman. She stands in stark contrast to the squeaky clean Joseph. Yet in this story, she is an actor—she determines what she wants and goes after it. She is persistent and consistent. She is focused and determined. When her plans are thwarted, she shifts gears and makes another plan. She is not undone by rejection—she keeps on keeping on!

Mrs. Potiphar's story may be a device to show how God's chosen one overcomes all obstacles and emerges victorious. She may or may not be a historical figure. Her episode is needed for Joseph to become a hero. Her role is to show that nothing can keep God's will from going forth. In the midst of adversity, the hero remains faithful and steadfast. Joseph exemplifies impeccable character. The combination of personal integrity and God's favor is one that will achieve great things.

Mrs. Potiphar may be a foil for Joseph's trek to power. She is often pitied because she is unfaithful to her husband. She is willing to sacrifice an innocent man to avenge her hurt ego and libido. She is one of few women in the Bible who have sex for reasons having nothing to do with procreation (Delilah is another).

In reality, she is a strong woman—focused, powerful, sexually liberated. Within patriarchy, she is a dangerous woman. We do not know enough about her story to understand her motivations. We do not know, for instance, what her relationship with her husband was like. We do not know what she did to occupy her time. We do not know if she has children or desires them. We do not know if she was especially attracted to Joseph (he was handsome and good-looking!) or if adultery was a pattern of life for her. We do not know whether she had had other lovers or what happened to them. We do not know if Joseph flirted with her or led her on in some way. The purpose of the story is to create a model hero. Joseph's story is a classic hero quest. And he needs Mrs. Potiphar to make the point that he is worthy of God's favor. Despite her action, she plays a positive role in Joseph's life and quest.

This story would hold special appeal for Israel. The Israelites saw themselves as underdogs on the world stage. On their own, they had no reason to think that they could conquer the world and institute a new religion. The odds were against them. Yet God called them and appointed them to be a light to the nations. And what God has for them will be theirs. There may be obstacles along the way, but God is in control and will bring the divine will into being. The Israelites were outside the established cultures, and their success is achieved in roundabout ways. Their history is marked by miracles and impossible victories. God was truly with them. In these ways, Joseph's story reflects Israel's story.

Looked at in this context, Potiphar's wife is not a villain. She serves a historical purpose that has little to do with who or what she is as a human being. She represents modern women who strive to be counted and recognized as full human beings. Her drive is highlighted. Women today continue to struggle with gaining respect in a culture that sees them as sexual objects or as wicked women for expressing their sexuality. Mrs. Potiphar is more than a foil for Joseph. She is a woman who, in a more equal world, might have assumed the job her husband had. She might have been a power broker in politics or industry. Her persistence and drive would have propelled her into the seats of power and influence.

REFLECTION QUESTIONS

1. Potiphar's wife is portrayed as sexually aggressive. What is the difference between being sexually liberated and sexually aggressive? What is the difference between being sexually liberated and promiscuous?

2. What are the implications of Mrs. Potiphar's story for issues of sexual harassment? How should such cases be handled?

3. It is speculated that Mrs. Potiphar lived a life of comfort and ease. She may have been bored. What do you do when you are bored?

4. What power and authority do you have? How do you express them? Explain.

5. What kind of support should be given to rape victims? Be specific.

6. There are numerous cases of women married to wealthy and powerful men who neglect or ignore them. How should these women handle their situations?

7. What should men who are married to inattentive, powerful women do? How do the actions of men differ from women in the same situations?

8. What should one do if one is dissatisfied with a spouse or partner? Be specific.

9. Our culture has a greater tolerance and acceptance of adultery than the Israelites did. Is adultery ever justified? Explain.

6

DELILAH: ENEMY OR ENTREPRENEUR?

$\mathcal{D}$elilah is a major player in the Samson saga. She is the instrument of his downfall; at least, that is the popular interpretation.

Samson was the last judge in Israel. When Israel was emancipated from Egyptian slavery, the nation was ruled by God through Moses, who was succeeded by Joshua. After Samson, Israel was ruled by kings—first Saul, then David, Solomon, and others. The judges represented a transition period in Israel's history. The judges were twelve persons who assumed military leadership in times of political crisis. Judges were also keepers of the faith for the nation. Ironically, Israel's first ruler after Joshua was Judah (remember his interactions with Tamar?). Among the twelve judges, one woman is named— Deborah. For a glimpse of her administration, read Judges 4–5.

By the end of Samson's saga, Israel had hit rock bottom in its social and religious decline. We meet Samson in Judges 13. His beginnings reach back to those of other biblical persons—his father, Manoah, is married to a barren woman who learns through divine means that she will conceive and deliver a son. God has a special mission for the lad. He is to begin the emancipation of Israel from Philistine captivity. (Read Judges 13:1–5.)

The son is to be a "nazirite," or one who is separated or consecrated to God. This implies special service to God.

> God spoke to Moses, saying: Speak to the Israelites and say to them: When either men or women make a special vow, the vow of a nazirite, to separate themselves to God, they shall separate themselves from wine and strong drink; they shall drink no wine vinegar or other vinegar, and shall not drink any grape juice or eat grapes, fresh or dried. All their days as nazirites they shall eat nothing that is produced by the grapevine, not even the seeds or the skins. All the days of their nazirite vow no razor shall come upon the head; until the time is completed for which they separate themselves to God, they shall be holy; they shall let the locks of the head grow long. All the days that they separate themselves to God they shall not go near a corpse. Even if their father or mother, brother or sister, should die, they may not defile themselves; because their consecration to God is upon the head. All their days as nazirites they are holy to God. (Num. 6:1–8)

Unlike some wives in the biblical record, Mrs. Manoah tells her husband about the revelation. Later, Mr. and Mrs. Manoah receive instructions from God's angel concerning their son's upbringing and destiny. She bears the son and names him Samson. God blesses the child. It is clear that God expects great things from Samson—and we are intrigued.

The first step toward disappointment is Samson's desire for a Philistine woman at Timnah. He commands his parents to get the woman for him because he is attracted to her. They protest because to do his bidding would violate the covenant with God to avoid marriages with foreign women. The narrator, however, states that the mixed marriage is ordained by God.

Samson's next action continues down the path of disappointment: he convinces his parents to accompany him to Timnah to get this bride-to-be. While at the vineyards of Timnah (it is not clear whether he drank any wine), he is attacked by a lion, which he kills with his bare hands. Samson is a man of obvious strength. His parents do not know of the attack.

Samson meets his heart's desire, and his parents return home. Later, Samson goes back to Timnah to get married. He remembers the lion and takes a side trip to check out the carcass. Why? We do not know! A swarm of bees has produced honey in the dead animal; Samson eats some and later offers some to his parents, who also eat. By doing so, he violates the nazirite vow not to eat unclean food; the honey is in the ritually unclean carcass and is also considered unclean. Again, his parents are uninformed about the source of the honey.

At the wedding feast, Samson is having a great time being the man of the hour. Samson bets the wedding party that no one can solve a riddle:

> "Out of the eater came something to eat.
> Out of the strong came something sweet." (Judg. 14:14)

If they cannot solve it, they will owe him thirty linen garments and thirty festal garments. If they solve it, Samson will owe them the same. Samson is confident that they will never guess the answer because it was the honey-filled carcass of the lion he killed earlier. No one but Samson knew this. On the fourth day of the seven-day feast, Samson's wedding party companions force his wife to find out the solution. If she fails, she and her father's house will be burned. The frightened, weeping woman tries to get the answer from him. Samson arrogantly refuses to tell her: "So Samson's wife wept before him, saying, 'You hate me; you do not really love me. You have asked a riddle of my people, but you have not explained it to me.' He said to her, 'Look, I have not told my father or my mother. Why should I tell you?'" (Judg. 14:16).

She continues to nag him, and he finally reveals the answer to her. She tells the guests, and they present their answer to Samson in the form of a riddle of their own. Samson knows he has been duped and betrayed by his new wife:

> The men of the town said to him on the seventh day before
> the sun went down,
> "What is sweeter than honey?
> What is stronger than a lion?"
> And he said to them,
> "If you had not plowed with my heifer,
> you would not have found out my riddle." (Judg. 14:18)

Samson is livid! He expresses his anger by killing thirty men in neighboring Ashkelon. He takes their garments and uses them to pay off his riddle debt. Still enraged, he goes back home without his wife. Her father assumes that Samson has divorced her, and her father gives her as wife to the best man at Samson's wedding. It is not clear by what authority the father did this, since Samson had not officially divorced her. Samson's nameless wife is powerless in the situation. Samson is depicted as an arrogant, violent, angry man. His actions are not done on behalf of his people or on behalf of God. He acts out of his anger and resentment.

Sometime later, Samson goes back to Timnah to visit his wife and finds out that she has been given to another man. Again, Samson acts out of anger and burns the grain, olive groves, and grape fields of the Philistines. In retaliation, the men of Timnah kill Samson's wife and her father. Without mercy, Samson kills a bunch of them: "Samson said to them, 'If this is what you do, I swear I will not stop until I have taken revenge on you.' He struck them down hip and thigh with great slaughter; and he went down and stayed in the cleft of the rock of Etam" (Judg. 15:7–8).

Things have really gotten out of hand; neither Samson nor the Philistines will back down. The Philistines raid Lehi in Judah because they want to get Samson for his destructive violence toward them. Although Samson is a judge, a government official, if you will, the men of Judah turn him over to the Philistines in order to save themselves. When the Philistines rush to meet him, Samson breaks free of his binding. He finds the jawbone of a donkey and uses it to kill one thousand Philistines. A second time, Samson touches an unclean thing; the jawbone was part of a dead animal.

> Samson said,
> "With the jawbone of a donkey,

heaps upon heaps,
with the jawbone of a donkey
I have slain a thousand men." (Judg. 15:16)

Samson arrogantly brags about his exploits. Yet he prays to God and acknowledges God's hand in his "victory." Further, Samson prays for water, and God grants his prayer. We are told that Samson judged Israel for twenty years. We are not told how his administration fared.

We next see Samson in Gaza, where he has a sexual encounter with a prostitute. The Philistines do not relent in their efforts to get Samson. They learn that he is with a prostitute, and they wait all night to ambush him. They plan to kill him in the morning. But Samson fools them by leaving at midnight. His escape includes taking the doors of the city gate and two posts. He carries them to the top of the hill in front of Hebron—an act designed to show the Philistines who he is! The city gate doors symbolize a city's defense, strength, and power. The power of Samson's God will replace the power of the Philistines.

Now, we prepare to meet Delilah. We have taken a long time to set forth Samson's story because it will help us to more fully understand the importance of his relationship with Delilah.

Samson is the most hated man in the land of the Philistines. He has wreaked havoc upon the Philistines. He has mocked them and destroyed their property and future livelihood. He has callously killed their kinsmen. He has taken advantage of their women. The Philistines will stop at nothing to finally bring down the self-important, ferocious, crazy Israelite! Their anger toward him is immense—they want to humiliate the despised Samson—and they intend to get him by any means necessary.

"After this he fell in love with a woman in the valley of Sorek, whose name was Delilah" (Judg. 16:4). Delilah is a woman whose identity is not tied to a man. There is no information given about her father or mother or any brothers, uncles, husband, or son. As such, she is an independent woman making her own way in the world. Further, the site of her home gives no clue about her family or nationality. The Valley of Sorek is in the Israelite territory within the land of Canaan. We cannot know with certainty whether she is a Philistine, Canaanite, or Israelite woman. Given Samson's attraction to foreign women, we assume that she is Canaanite. And Samson loves her.

Samson has not been known to love wisely, so we are intrigued that after a one-night stand with a different woman, he is now in love. We do not know the circumstances of their initial meeting. He saw his first wife from afar and lusted after her. He saw a prostitute in Gaza and slept with her. We do not know if he is being impulsive or if this may be the "real thing."

We are not told whether Delilah loves him. She knows that he is a wanted man, and his presence puts her in danger. The story unfolds: "The lords of the Philistines came to her and said to her, 'Coax him, and find out what makes his strength so great, and how we may overpower him, so that we may bind him in order to subdue him; and we will each give you eleven hundred pieces of silver" (Judg. 16:5).

The leaders of the Philistines make her an offer she cannot refuse—the secret to Samson's great strength in exchange for eleven hundred pieces of silver from each of the leaders. We do not know how many leaders approach her. She could be really, really rich! Samson's wife had been threatened with death; Delilah is offered a huge sum for her help. She agrees to the deal. (Read Judges 16:6–9.)

Delilah does not use her "feminine wiles" to trick Samson into a confession. She asks him point-blank. She sees no need to beat around the bush; she wants to know and she asks. There is no deception in her inquiry and no evidence, so far, that she used sexual power to find out the secret to his strength. Samson, on the other hand, does not take her question seriously. He deceives her; he tells her that if he is tied up with seven fresh bowstrings, he will be rendered weak as a lamb. The Philistines bring the bowstrings, and Delilah ties Samson up with them. We are not told whether Samson consented to be tied up or whether he has fallen asleep first. We presume he is asleep. Delilah tells him that he is about to be overtaken by the Philistines, upon which he breaks free.

The game continues. Delilah does not change her tactic and is direct with Samson. He does not question her desire to know his secret. He seems unaware that the Philistines are hiding nearby. He seems focused only on this game with Delilah. (Read Judges 16:10–12.)

She takes new ropes and binds him; but again, he easily breaks free. A third time, they play the game. A third time, Delilah is direct with her request. This time, Samson tells her that if his hair is braided into seven locks and pinned, he will be weak. But again, he fools her. (Read Judges 16:13–14.)

This time, we are told that Samson was asleep when Delilah tries his answer. The tension is building—exasperation is setting in for Delilah and us! Samson seems unbothered by her tenacity.

The fourth time, Delilah changes her strategy. She must get the answer so that she can be paid. She appeals to his emotions:

> Then she said to him, "How can you say, 'I love you,' when your heart is not with me? You have mocked me three times now and have not told me what makes your strength so great." Finally, after she had nagged him with her words day after day, and pestered him, he was tired to death. So he told her his whole secret, and said to her, "A razor has never come upon my head; for I

have been a nazirite to God from my mother's womb. If my head were shaved, then my strength would leave me; I would become weak, and be like anyone else." (Judg. 16:15–17)

If Samson loves her, he will stop playing games and reveal the secret of his strength. Never once does he ask why she wants to know. Never once does he suspect her motives. He keeps visiting her and, presumably, having sex with her. We are not told whether Delilah is a prostitute; the text does not say. We may not assume that she is. However, Samson never proposes marriage nor does he offer payments for services rendered. They seem to have a relationship based on a level of mutuality and pleasure. The text does not reveal anything to indicate Delilah's desire to be married or to have children. They both seem to be consenting adults. After constantly nagging and pestering Samson, Delilah wears him down. An ominous note is struck when Samson tells her "his whole secret." To shave his head is to make him weak. His confession is sincere and earnest. This time, Delilah knows she has hit pay dirt. The text does not record any moments of tenderness between the two. Samson has poured out his whole heart, and Delilah seals the deal with the leaders of the Philistines, who show her the money!

Samson falls asleep, and an unnamed man shaves off Samson's seven locks of hair. Immediately, he begins to weaken and lose his strength. When Delilah sounds the alarm that the Philistines are upon him, he thinks he can respond with his usual strength. But God had left him. "So the Philistines seized him and gouged out his eyes. They brought him down to Gaza and bound him with bronze shackles; and he ground at the mill in the prison" (Judg. 16:21).

Delilah disappears and is silent in the rest of the story. Some speculate that she moved to the coast with the money she received. But we can only speculate—we have no information.

Samson is captured at long last. The Philistines have gouged out his eyes and imprisoned him. He is thoroughly degraded and humiliated. They arrange for Samson to be the entertainment in the temple of Dagon, a Canaanite god, before some three thousand Philistine men and women. Samson prays to God to give him strength for one last act of revenge. Samson grasps two pillars and pulls them down. The entire temple collapses and kills the Philistines and Samson! He is buried in his family's cemetery.

Samson seems never to understand his true mission of providing leadership for his people. He enjoys one-upmanship games, evident in his love of riddles. He uses his knowledge as power over others. He is an emotional, impulsive man who cannot control his temper. He acts first and does not think at all. His character flaws are his undoing—yet Delilah is blamed for his downfall.

Tradition has portrayed Delilah as a nagging, flirtatious woman who over-powers Samson with her sexual allure. The text, however, does not character-ize her in that way. She does not trick Samson. She asks a straightforward ques-tion, and he eventually answers it. Samson spends a lot of time at Delilah's home, but she does not seem to coerce or otherwise seduce him. We are told very little about their encounters. She makes herself available to Samson for reasons we are not given. We infer that they have a sexual arrangement because of Samson's sleeping and waking, but no details are given.

In Delilah, we find an impressive independent woman. She sees the Philis-tine offer as a way of securing her financial future. Since we have no informa-tion about her emotions, we do not know whether she regretted turning Samson over to the Philistine leaders. We know only that she was paid hand-somely for her work with Samson. In her, we find a woman who knew an easy mark when she saw one. She took the money and ran.

If Delilah was a Philistine, then her loyalty would naturally align with her people. She would be as disgusted with Samson as the Philistine leaders were. The Israelites were not held in high esteem among the Philistines. They were pesky and arrogant; they plundered and murdered and demolished property. The Israelites seemed bent on destroying the Philistines.

Whatever her allegiance, Delilah is a powerful and dangerous woman. She exercises great power over Samson simply by being straightforward and direct. It is not her fault or her responsibility that Samson loves her and is willing to reveal the secret of his strength. Samson tries to use his knowledge to control others. Delilah obtains the knowledge she needs for overpowering him. Samson always has the choice to hand over the information Delilah wants or to withhold it. When challenged on his love, Samson always gives in. Why he reveals his secrets to women is not known, but in every case, he makes a choice to share them. It has been said that knowledge is power—more power to Delilah!

A popular lesson from this story is never to love anyone totally. To love fully, openly, and honestly is to sign your death warrant. Too often, men are told not to give their hearts to women. They are told it is better for them to play the field and avoid commitment. To be honest and loving with women is to make a man weak and powerless. This kind of thinking places the blame for Samson's downfall on Delilah. The blame rightly belongs on Samson, who cared more for himself than the nation he was consecrated to serve and lead. His weaknesses of uncontrollable anger, vicious violence, self-absorbed arro-gance, and sexual obsession rendered him unable to think and act in the best interest of his people.

Delilah, of course, can be accused of being a selfish traitor. Nothing is said of Samson's kinsmen who attempt to turn him over to the Philistines, but

Delilah has committed a crime against the state. She claims no loyalty to Samson or his God, however. The scheme to capture Samson is the work of the Philistine leaders, not Delilah. They seek to use her; but they are willing to pay her for it. Samson is not shown providing any money or matrimony. She is an unattached woman. We do not know who she is or to what she is committed. She owes nothing to Samson except what they have agreed upon. Delilah is a woman trying to make it within the limits of her world. She is willing to interact with a known felon and fugitive. She sees an opportunity to secure her future and takes it. Because she is not attached to any man, she needs to establish a solid pension plan. The money she earns from the Philistine leaders would provide a nice sum for her 401(k) account. She loves herself enough to look ahead.

According to popular notions, Delilah's story serves the patriarchy well. Her story says to men, "Watch out for those foreign women; they will destroy men every time. Use women, but do not fall in love with them. Love women, and they will betray you!" Another look shows that Delilah is a woman who is looking out for herself in a world where her place is unknown. She dares to earn a living and provide a home without the assistance of men. She dares to enjoy sexual freedom without the burden of having children. She dares to make a place of her own. She dares to make deals that are advantageous to her.

For Israel, Delilah's story is symbolic of the depth to which the proud nation has fallen. Samson's downfall mirrors Israel's own. Samson's attraction to foreign women mirrors Israel's attraction to foreign gods. Samson's suicidal ending mirrors Israel's ending by its refusal to leave those foreign gods alone.

REFLECTION QUESTIONS

1. How do you characterize Delilah? How do you characterize Samson?
2. How can women be fully empowered beings? Is an intimate relationship with a man a requirement? Explain.
3. History recounts stories of women who align themselves with powerful men. What motivates them to do so? Are the motivations the same for men who align themselves with powerful women?
4. Some men are fearful of powerful and independent women. Of what are they afraid? Is their fear rational?
5. This story has been used by some men to avoid intimacy. What can be done to reverse this? Are the reasons to avoid intimacy the same for women who fear closeness?
6. Many women and men stay in unhealthy relationships. What can men and women do to establish and support healthier relationships?
7. Delilah is often portrayed as the femme fatale or the treacherous woman who aggressively uses her abundant sexuality and sensuality to render men impotent and powerless. Has this study of Delilah changed your perception of her? Explain.
8. Do you sympathize with Delilah and her choices? Explain.
9. In what ways are you like Delilah? In what ways are you like Samson?

7

JEZEBEL: DEVIOUS OR DIVA?

The very mention of Jezebel's name conjures up images of overdone makeup, excessive jewelry and perfume, expensive and inappropriately sexy clothes, and raw sensuality. Ask anyone, male or female, about Jezebel, and an opinion will be given. She is evil personified, and everyone despises her. Her handling of Elijah is legendary. Her handling of Naboth is infamous. Yet in many ways, Jezebel has gotten a bad rap.

Our previous Bible study hinted at a new era about to begin for Israel. The judges represented a transition in leadership and governance. The Israelites had settled in the hills of central Canaan and were in constant contact and conflict with the Canaanites who were already settled in the land. The book of Judges shows how Israel struggled to hold its own, both religiously and politically, in a place where the Israelites were different and not welcomed. The book ends on a somber note: "In those days there was no king in Israel; all the people did what was right in their own eyes" (Judg. 21:25).

Israel was in really bad shape. We learn of Israel's transition and history in six books: First and Second Samuel, First and Second Kings, and First and Second Chronicles. All of these books are part of the D tradition and introduce the office of the prophet. The prophets played important roles in the life of Israel: they were a liaison between human beings and God. True prophets challenged Israelite leaders and people to stay faithful and obedient to God's covenant. They were keepers of Israel's moral, religious, and ethical standards.

A true prophet (Hebrew *nabi*) is one who is called by God. In the D tradition, prophets were real or true, mediated between God and people, and mediated between kings and people in certain cases. The prophet's role varied throughout Israel's history. Some supported the monarchy; others opposed it. In whatever way they related to the monarchy, prophets were part of the society; they were not detached representatives for God. The trials and triumphs were as much a part of their lives as they were for the people. The prophets were acquainted with the basics of Israelite history and theology. They all believed, for example, that Israel had been specially chosen by God. Israel was in a covenantal relationship with God that conferred blessings and obligations. Most prophets believed that Israel failed to keep its end of the bargain and therefore caused its own destruction. Israel sought other gods, ignored social justice issues, and behaved badly. God had no choice but to allow its downfall. The prophets also believed that true repentance would restore the breach in the covenant and restore the nation as God's chosen people. A general schema of Israel's monarchical history follows:

> First and Second Samuel give a picture of Israel's early experience of the monarchy. These books trace Samuel's role in discerning and anointing Saul as the first king. They tell of David's stormy but charismatic rise to king. David's administration symbolizes Israel at its best. All aspects of life—social, religious, economic, political—came together in the person of David, the apple of God's eye.
> First and Second Kings continue the monarchy history. First Kings begins with David's death and Solomon's ascension to the throne and traces the monarchical line to the Exile. After Solomon's death, the nation was split into two kingdoms: Judah (capital city in Jerusalem) in the south, and Israel (capital city in Samaria) in the north. Each had a string of kings, none of whom equaled David. The theme of these two books is Israel's failure to live up to God's expectations of it. The people strayed from God and were cut off from their roots and their source of life. Each king was evaluated by how well or how poorly he kept the covenantal obligations.
> First and Second Chronicles trace Israel's history from Adam to the end of the Exile. The emphasis is on David and Solomon as fulfilling God's will for a central worship place at Jerusalem.

The D tradition called for absolute and exclusive loyalty to God; any wavering meant disaster.

Jezebel is a prominent figure in the life of Elijah, who prophesied during the reign of Ahab. Ahab ruled in the Northern Kingdom (Israel); he was the seventh king after Solomon's death. Ahab's administration was marked by military strength and governmental stability. The focus of his story is his confrontations with Elijah, the prophet: the first was on Mount Carmel, where Elijah challenged the prophets of the Canaanite god, Baal, to end the drought (1 Kings 18:17–40); the second occurred when Ahab sought advice from two unnamed prophets (1 Kings 20:13–22); the third occurred when Ahab went to claim the deceased Naboth's vineyard (1 Kings 21); and the fourth was during Ahab's battle against the Arameans, where he died (1 Kings 22). Ahab is harshly evaluated not because of his record, but because of his wife, Jezebel, who worshiped Baal.

Elijah was from a small town, Tishbe, in Gilead. His mission was to destroy the cult of Baal in Israel. Baalism was already in the land when the Israelites moved there. But it was gaining momentum within the Israelite culture through the arranged and politically motivated marriage between Israel's King Omri's son, Ahab, and Tyrian King Ethbaal's daughter, Jezebel. In other words, Jezebel brought her religion with her to the capital city of Samaria. From Samaria, the religion spread like wildfire in a land already under the influence of Baal worship.

Baal was part of the Canaanite religious system of which the god El was the head. Baal was a fertility god that also controlled the weather (rainfall, sunshine, storms, etc.). The people outside the city limits would find Baal attractive as they prayed for optimal agricultural conditions.

Elijah challenged the people to forget and to resist Baal. For Israelites, there is and could be only one God. Elijah was zealous for God and tried to get his people to understand and claim his conviction. Failure to embrace exclusive devotion and loyalty to God would result in destruction and disaster. With this brief overview, it is time to meet Jezebel.

We are introduced to Jezebel in 1 Kings 16:29–33:

> In the thirty-eighth year of King Asa of Judah, Ahab son of Omri began to reign over Israel; Ahab son of Omri reigned over Israel in Samaria twenty-two years. Ahab son of Omri did evil in the sight of God more than all who were before him. And as if it had been a light thing for him to walk in the sins of Jeroboam son of Nebat, he took as his wife Jezebel daughter of King Ethbaal of the Sidonians, and went and served Baal, and worshiped him. He erected an altar for Baal in the house of Baal, which he built in Samaria. Ahab also made a sacred pole. Ahab did more to provoke the anger of God, the God of Israel, than had all the kings of Israel who were before him.

It was not unusual for men to marry for political reasons. Such marriages connected and strengthened families so that military and political alliances would be sealed. That was the case with Ahab and Jezebel.

During Omri's administration, Israel enjoyed a measure of political and economic stability. For fifty years prior to that, Israel struggled with its neighbors. Damascus was the biggest threat to Israelite security. Damascus and Tyre had a treaty agreement at some point, and the alliance made Damascus an even bigger threat. Damascus had taken over some Israelite border towns. In addition, Assyria was gaining power.

Omri came into power at a time when Israel needed immediate help as well as a long-range plan. He established a new capital at Samaria, which Ahab completed. He sought internal harmony, a peaceful relationship with Judah, alliance with the Phoenicians, and military strength east of the Jordan River. The Tyre-Damascus alliance had broken down. Omri forged an alliance with Ethbaal, king of the Phoenician city of Tyre, and Ethbaal married off his daughter to Omri's son. Tyre itself was a strong city with controlling interests in a number of other cities and provided wholesale and retail outlets for Israel's agricultural production. An alliance with Tyre was advantageous for Israel for military and commercial reasons. Further, Tyre benefited from the alliance in that it now had an another ally against an increasingly threatening Damascus. In addition, close ties with Israel opened up commercial opportunities in the southern region of the land. Such alliances were between equals, each bringing something of substance to the table (see pp. 243–48 of John Bright's reference in Resources section).

Although Israel enjoyed political and economic stability, the religious scene took a turn for the worse. When the marriage between Ahab and Jezebel was sealed, it was expected that she and her people would continue to worship their deities, Baal and Asherah. As a sign of respect, Ahab built a temple to Baal and a shrine to Asherah in Samaria. There was nothing unusual about the arrangement (Solomon did the same for his wives). Baal and the one true God of Israel coexisted.

As I stated earlier, Baal worship may have been attractive to people who worked the land and needed favorable weather conditions, especially rain, in order for the crops to prosper. Furthermore, we know from Samson's story that many of the Canaanites stayed in the cities and towns that Israel conquered. They would have acknowledged Israel's God but would probably continue to worship their own gods. So, within Israel, there was already Baal worship. Jezebel's desire to extend Baal worship throughout the land would be cause for alarm for the Israelites. Jezebel was an enthusiastic follower of Baal, and she made sure that her devotion was widely known. As part of her royal prerogative, Jezebel was killing off God's prophets and causing great fear among them: "Now Obadiah revered God greatly; when Jezebel was killing off the prophets of God, Obadiah took a hundred prophets, hid them fifty to a cave, and provided them with bread and water" (1 Kings 18:3–4).

In an earlier scene, Elijah had predicted a drought in the land. The point was to prove that God, not Baal, was in charge of the needed rainfall. After some time, God told Elijah to go to Ahab to inform him that God would end the drought. Ahab had been looking for Elijah ever since his predictions about the drought. When the two meet, Ahab calls him the "troubler of Israel" (1 Kings 18:17–18). Elijah corrects him—Ahab is the real troubler of Israel because he has forsaken the true God and followed Baal. There is no evidence that Ahab was a staunch follower of either God or Baal; if he believed in God, it was a marginal belief.

A large number of Israelites were probably ambivalent and content to serve two deities: "Elijah then came near to all the people, and said, 'How long will you go limping with two different opinions? If Yahweh is God, follow Yahweh; but if Baal, then follow Baal.' The people did not answer him a word" (1 Kings 18:21).

On Mount Carmel, where Ahab summons "all the Israelites" (meaning all men!) along with the 450 prophets of Baal and the 400 prophets of Asherah, Elijah referees a battle between Baal and God. Two bulls are cut into pieces and placed on sticks of wood. The prophets of Baal call upon their deity, and Elijah calls upon God. Whoever responds with fire will be deemed the superior and one true God. The prophets of Baal feverishly appeal to their god, who does not respond. Elijah mocks them and makes them look foolish (1 Kings 18:26–29). Then Elijah appeals to his God, who responds magnificently (1 Kings 18:36–38).

The people are convinced that Elijah's God is the One, and they worship God. Elijah's mission seems accomplished. But his job is not yet finished. He seizes the prophets of Baal and Asherah and kills them, just as Jezebel had done to the prophets of God. Shortly afterward, the rains come.

So astonishing are these events that Ahab cannot wait to tell Jezebel. She is back at home, which is her rightful place according to patriarchy. Jezebel is outraged that Elijah has killed the prophets she has been supporting. She sends a message to him: "So may the gods do to me, and more also, if I do not make your life like the life of one of them by this time tomorrow" (1 Kings 19:2).

Elijah fears Jezebel's threat and runs into the desert beyond Beer-sheba to Mount Horeb, where he sulks, pouts, and whines. To be candid, Elijah has reason to be afraid. Jezebel's campaign to place Baalism front and center in Israel is being compromised by Elijah's opposition. She has already shown that she has the power to kill. They both have the power to support their respective prophets and the power to destroy the opposition. Jezebel's zeal for Baal has driven Elijah's cohorts underground—literally! (See 1 Kings 18:4.) Elijah's zeal after the Mount Carmel incident effectively challenges Jezebel's power and authority. The stage is set for a real showdown between the two.

While on Horeb, Elijah is told by God to hang tough. God has saved a remnant of seven thousand in Israel who are faithful (1 Kings 19:18). Both Jezebel and Elijah disappear from the story and do not reappear until 1 Kings 21.

The scene opens with Ahab seeking to acquire a vineyard owned by Naboth, a resident of Jezreel. Ahab wants the land, which is situated near the royal home in Jezreel, for a vegetable garden. Naboth refuses because the land is the property of his ancestors. As such, the land is not Naboth's to sell or exchange—it belongs to his family, past and future. Ahab is distraught because he knows that Naboth is within his rights to hold on to his land. Ahab is so disturbed that he goes home, takes to his bed, pouts, and refuses to eat (Elijah exhibited similar behavior when he fled from Jezebel). And guess who reappears? Yes, Jezebel:

His wife Jezebel came to him and said, "Why are you so depressed that you will not eat?" He said to her, "Because I spoke to Naboth the Jezreelite and said to him, 'Give me your vineyard for money; or else, if you prefer, I will give you another vineyard for it'; but he answered, 'I will not give you my vineyard.'" His wife Jezebel said to him, "Do you now govern Israel? Get up, eat some food, and be cheerful; I will give you the vineyard of Naboth the Jezreelite." (1 Kings 21:5–7)

Jezebel, a strong woman, takes over! She expresses concern about her husband's demeanor and asks him why he is so depressed. This scene shows her to be a caring and concerned wife, contrary to some commentators' assessment. She is amazed and appalled at the situation. She chastises Ahab; after all, he is the king. She has clear opinions about prerogatives of royalty. Ahab needs to get a clue, so she helps him out. She tells him to stop worrying, to get up, to eat something, and to make a happy face—she will take care of everything.

She fashions a plan and enlists the help of others to execute (pun intended!) it. (Read 1 Kings 21:8–14.)

Her plan affirms that she knows, understands, and accepts Israelite law and custom:

➤ She knows that if Naboth has no heirs, especially male heirs, the vineyard will revert to the king.
➤ She places Ahab's official seal on her letter (remember Judah's signet?).
➤ She sends the letter to the men with the authority to carry out her wishes.
➤ She knows the importance of using the occasion of a fast to implement her plan. A fast was called so that a gathering of powerful men could make major decisions for the community.
➤ She knows that Israelite law requires two witnesses to bring charges.
➤ She knows the penalty for cursing the king and God is stoning to death.

Further, Jezebel is astute enough to know that the leaders will implement her plan out their own self-interest. The royal home in Jezreel is an important source of income and employment and prestige for the city. If Ahab moves his home elsewhere, the city will lose money and status. To protect the city, the leaders are willing to sacrifice one of their prominent citizens. They follow her instructions to the letter.

There is only one thing left to do—share the good news with Ahab: "As soon as Jezebel heard that Naboth had been stoned and was dead, Jezebel said to Ahab, 'Go, take possession of the vineyard of Naboth the Jezreelite, which he refused to give you for money; for Naboth is not alive, but dead.' As soon as Ahab heard that Naboth was dead, Ahab set out to go down to the vineyard of Naboth the Jezreelite, to take possession of it" (1 Kings 21:15–16).

No one expresses remorse at the deed. Jezebel has made Ahab's vegetable garden a reality. She uses her power and royal authority to do what her husband did not or could not do. Ahab does not question her; he simply sets out to take the vineyard. He has gotten what he wants, and that is the only thing that matters to him.

But this is all too easy. Elijah reappears! God sends Elijah to confront Ahab about this matter, and Elijah also predicts Ahab's demise. (Read 1 Kings 21:20–24.)

Ahab and his family will be utterly destroyed. And as for Jezebel, her death will be horrific. The narrator makes sure that we understand the seriousness of Ahab and Jezebel's transgression: "Indeed, there was no one like Ahab, who sold himself to do what was evil in the sight of God, urged on by his wife Jezebel. He acted most abominably in going after idols, as the Amorites had done, whom God drove out before the Israelites" (1 Kings 21:25–26).

After hearing Elijah's indictment, Ahab is repentant. God delays the disastrous end. The account of Ahab's death is recorded in 1 Kings 22:29–40.

Jezebel's death scene has been the fuel for much of the negative perception of her. The monarchical line after Ahab included Ahaziah, Jehoram, and Jehu. One of Jehu's tasks was to rid Israel of Baal worship, once and for all. Jehu was anointed as king by an emissary of Elisha, who succeeded Elijah. By destroying Ahab's house, Jehu effectively ended Israel's alliance with Tyre, and it was hoped that Baal worship would be ended. In order for Israel to move forward, all traces of Baalism needed to be purged. Jehu had the task of making sure that Jezebel, his political and religious opponent, was destroyed.

When Jezebel hears that Jehu is in Jezreel (she maintained the royal home there after Ahab's death), she prepares herself for death. She paints her eyes, adorns her head, and perches herself in a window. Her actions have been misinterpreted. Some think she is trying to seduce Jehu so that he will not kill her. She is really letting Jehu and everybody else know that even in the face of death, she is still a queen—a diva, if you will! If she is to die, it will be as royalty and not a frightened, crazed person. She will be in control, even in her demise:

> When Jehu came to Jezreel, Jezebel heard of it; she painted her eyes, and adorned her head, and looked out of the window. As Jehu entered the gate, she said, "Is it peace, Zimri, murderer of your master?" He looked up to the window and said, "Who is on my side? Who?" Two or three eunuchs looked out at him. He said, "Throw her down." So they threw her down; some of her blood spattered on the wall and on the horses, which trampled on her. Then

he went in and ate and drank; he said, "See to that cursed woman and bury her; for she is a king's daughter." But when they went to bury her, they found no more of her than the skull and the feet and the palms of her hands. When they came back and told him, he said, "This is the word of God, which God spoke by God's servant Elijah the Tishbite, 'In the territory of Jezreel the dogs shall eat the flesh of Jezebel; the corpse of Jezebel shall be like dung on the field in the territory of Jezreel, so that no one can say, This is Jezebel.'" (2 Kings 9:30–37)

"Zimri" is a reference to a military man who assassinated King Elah to assume the throne in Israel. He ruled for one week, then committed suicide. Jezebel feels that the situation between Jehu and her is like that of Zimri and Elah. She insults him even though he is about to kill her. Ms. Diva is still in control! After her servants push her from the window, Jehu is so unmoved and unconcerned that he eats a meal. As an afterthought, he instructs the servants to bury her out respect for her royal background. But all they find are her skull, her feet, and the palms of her hands. In other words, Jezebel has finally been destroyed. And we are left with this horrid end to her story. So, what are we to make of her story?

As a starting point, we need to understand that her story fits in the larger body of scripture shaped within the D tradition. Israel's history in this tradition is measured against Israel's faithfulness (or faithlessness) to the instructions and teachings in the book of Deuteronomy. Israel is required to worship only God. There can be no ambivalence or waffling about this worship. The tradition recognizes that other religions and other gods exist, but Israel is to remain pure and unaffected by them.

Although both Israelite and Canaanite farmers would be concerned about favorable agricultural conditions, they believed their fortunes were tied to very different gods. For both, the cycle of growth, harvest, death, and regrowth was rooted in the rhythms of farm life. The fruitfulness of the earth paralleled the rhythms of human life. For the Canaanites, fruitfulness of the land was closely tied to sexuality. Canaanite gods and goddesses were thought to be actively involved in the life rhythms of human beings and nature. A weather god, therefore, would be extremely important. Baal, the god of rain and storms, would be a major deity. The male Baal had a female counterpart (in most cases, she is called Asherah; in others, she is Astarte). These deities were also sexual beings whose sex lives determined good or bad agricultural conditions. It is not clear to what extent Baal worship incorporated sexual relations. The biblical account is too skewed toward the negative to be a reliable source. But the appeal for favorable growing conditions would be attractive to Israelite farmers. After all, the Canaanite gods had done well for the Canaanites, who were renowned farmers.

For Israelite farmers, if Baal could make a difference, so be it. If God pitched in to help, so much the better. Yet the prophets tried to convince the people that God was sufficient. God was the God who controlled everything. All other gods were pretenders, not contenders. Absolute allegiance to God would result in abundant blessings. The prophets' task was to help the people hold God above all others. The prophets' sermons foreshadowed a popular image of God in the African American church tradition: God is so wide, we cannot get around; so high, we cannot get over; so deep, we cannot get under!

For the prophets, this God is superior to all the other gods and goddesses put together. This God called a tiny, unlikely Israel to rule the world; not for fame and glory, but to be an example of justice, harmony, unity, faith, and love. This God is the God because of what has been done with a motley crew of loosely affiliated tribes. If this weird collection can be transformed into a world power—ruling justly and humanely, ruling with concern for all of creation, ruling within the purview of the Divine—then this God can and will do anything we can imagine.

Anything that threatened Israel's ability or capacity to love God had to be destroyed and eliminated. Failure to express this deep loyalty would result in disaster and tragedy. Thus, we find throughout the Hebrew Scriptures warnings to stay away from foreign women. Although patriarchy is uneven in its treatment of such women, the D tradition makes such liaisons clearly troublesome. It was believed that foreign women would lure their Israelite husbands away from God to Baal. This view is extremely unflattering to the heroes of Israel's history; they appear weak, pliable, easily influenced, and wishy-washy. By implication, patriarchy gives great power to these women—they appear strong, determined, focused, persuasive, dangerous, compelling, and powerful.

Patriarchy would have us believe that these women are seductive in their use of power. The seductive nature of these women is implied in their capacity to sway God's chosen men from the course laid out for them. Love (or lust) makes these men weak and easily influenced. Patriarchy blames women for men's "weaknesses." Men who are fearless in battle, men who kill wild animals with their bare hands, men who take down giants with mere stones, men who launch massive building programs in enemy territory, men who judge fairly are all suddenly rendered wimpish under the attentions of women. According to patriarchy, men would rather blame women than own up to their character flaws and foibles. Patriarchy lets men off the hook; God, however, holds them accountable.

Among all the dangerous foreign women, Jezebel stands alone as the one most able to undermine Israel's faith. It is possible that everyday people liked her. She was regal, articulate, smart, sensitive, and generous. She was, after all, a princess before she became queen of Israel. Her father and grandfather were kings. It is likely that she grew up in the palace watching her mother and grandmother live out the duties of queen and queen mother. She was used to the finer things in life—the best foods and wines, the best clothing, the best furnishings. She was used to the best teachers and tutors. No doubt, she was privy to conversations around the dinner table where her daddy and his friends talked military and commercial strategies. She listened attentively as her dad set forth his policies and reforms. She watched her mom use her own power and authority with grace and poise. She watched her parents negotiate the terms of their marriage. I imagine she celebrated with her people at the festivals that celebrated Baal's blessings or entreated Baal's kindness. She sat with her mama and grandmama during the services at the Baal temple. She danced with her girlfriends at the shrine of Asherah. She helped the servants prepare the feasts her parents sponsored for the prophets of Baal and Asherah. Jezebel lived in a bubble of royal pride and privilege.

When Jezebel married Ahab, she did not get a sudden case of terminal amnesia. Instead, she brought her history and life with her to Israel. Her background had prepared her to be a Canaanite queen, and Israelite customs were a real eye-opener! She just could not understand the insecurity of the Israelite God: this God required absolute loyalty. This God required strict obedience. This God had a long list of do's and don'ts that even the greatest saints would find challenging. This God bragged about (and encouraged people to remember) deeds of valor and violence. All the while, God's prophets preached doom and gloom—they were very depressing.

Moreover, for Jezebel, Israel's God may have seemed incomplete—there was no female counterpart. Besides, Baal had been around longer—he had seniority. So, Jezebel saw nothing wrong with promoting her god. She was doing the bumbling Israelites a favor by providing a more reliable and less demanding god.

Jezebel was dangerous because she was "somebody" before she arrived in Israel. She was a woman of means and compared well with Elijah, her nemesis. As princess and queen, she brought royal privilege to her deeds. As God's "man" (Elijah was called "man of God"), Elijah brought divine privilege to his deeds. Jezebel was zealous for Baal; Elijah was zealous for God. Jezebel used her power to destroy the opposing prophets of God; Elijah used his power to destroy the opposing prophets of Baal.

Then, there was that situation with Naboth. The D tradition condemned her for Baal worship, which allowed folks to be ruthless. She was condemned on religious and ethical grounds, but she acted out of political motivations. In Jezebel's opinion, as king, Ahab was entitled to anything he wanted. Certainly if he was king of Tyre, he could just take the vineyard. Jezebel was impatient with Israelite law that gave ordinary folk the right to deny the king his desire. Ahab understood the importance of honoring each man within the culture. Ahab believed it enough to let the matter drop; he did not like the situation, but there was nothing he could do. Jezebel did not see things his way. She used the system that Israel lived under to deal with Naboth as if he were a Tyrian citizen. Insubordination was a capital offense punishable by death as far as she was concerned. Jezebel did not make the rules; she just used them.

The D tradition and patriarchy had no choice but to get rid of all traces of Jezebel. She was made the embodiment of Israel's disobedience and following of Baal. Because of the power for evil that the tradition assigned to her, it is easy to conclude that she would have to be dealt a harsh hand. An interesting point is that Jezebel and Elijah never had a face-to-face confrontation. They never interacted personally with each other. Perhaps a meeting would have been inappropriate since she was a woman. Yet they were similar: both were active, fanatical, violent, stubborn—and all in the name of their deities. And Jezebel had the nerve to stand up to Elijah. Israel's kings defied the prophets at considerable risk. Jezebel was not afraid of Elijah, and he knew it.

Because of her worship of Baal, the dreaded threat to Israel's well-being and connection to God, Jezebel *had* to die a horrible death. The description of her demise is the most graphic in the Bible and is not for the fainthearted: she was flung from a window; she was smashed to the ground and trampled upon by horses; her blood splattered; and her flesh was devoured!

She served patriarchy and the D tradition well. But Jezebel deserves another look. She was not a harlot or seductress. She was not involved in any sexual scenes. She was a woman from another culture and worldview trying to adjust in a new and strange land. She was not a villain to be eternally despised—she was religiously committed, politically savvy, determined, self-assured, bodacious, and clever. She was dedicated to her family and a zealous missionary for Baal. And she died as she lived—royally!

REFLECTION QUESTIONS

1. What is a "jezebel"? What makes a woman a "jezebel"? Does your definition conform to what you have just learned about Queen Jezebel?
2. It has been said, by women, that all women have a little Jezebel in them. Do you agree? Explain.
3. Does it surprise you to learn that Jezebel appears in no sexual scenes or even potentially sexual scenes in the Bible? How did the association between sexuality and Jezebel develop? What purpose does such a picture serve?
4. Foreign women play strong political roles in the Hebrew Scriptures (Potiphar's wife, Delilah, Jezebel, Tamar). What does patriarchy try to say to Israelite women through the stories of foreign women?
5. What is your notion of the ideal woman? Be specific. If you are a woman, do you fit your ideal?
6. What have you learned from Jezebel that is empowering for you?
7. Jezebel was a woman of great passions and gifts. What are some of your passions and gifts? Be specific.
8. Can you name examples of strong, smart women married to men who do not seem to be their equal? What motivates them to connect?
9. What can you do to encourage young women to be all they can be? What can you do to encourage young men to appreciate and love strong, smart women?
10. Jezebel has been slandered and destroyed because of her faith and power. What Christian parallels can you name?
11. Jezebel was thrust into an unfamiliar culture and expected to give up her previous life. What are the implications of her story for issues of hospitality, pluralism, and diversity?
12. Jezebel and Elijah were persons of great temper and anger. How can we and our leaders control our tempers and anger?
13. Would you name your daughter Jezebel? Explain.
14. Human beings have a tendency to condemn what they do not understand. How is this illustrated in Jezebel's story?
15. In the United States, persons are free to practice any religion they choose. What are the implications of interfaith choices for Christianity?
16. How do you deal with disappointment? Explain.
17. Have you given thought to how you wish to die? Why or why not?
18. Are you a selfish person? How is your selfishness expressed? What can you do about this?

8

JOB'S WIFE: FOE OR FOIL?

 *J*ob's wife utters one of the more infamous lines in the Bible! She is depicted as a faithless, cold, and cruel woman. Her tactic in the face of adversity seems to be surrender: throw in the towel, and forget about it. In view of Job's dilemma and its eventual resolution, we may want to reconsider her words. She may have been wiser than we thought.

The book of Job is often quoted. There are lovely lines of faith and hope within the story:

Job said, "Naked I came from my mother's womb, and naked shall I return there; God gave, and God has taken away; blessed be the name of God."(Job 1.21)

Shall we receive the good at the hand of God, and not receive the bad? (Job 2:10)

See, God will kill me; I have no hope;
but I will defend my ways to God's face. (Job 13:15)

We most often turn to Job to comfort those who labor under undeserved suffering. We tout Job as an example of one with unending patience. We lift up Job as a paragon of faithful living. Yet in most of this, we have misrepresented the point of Job's story. We have approached this book seeking the answer to a basic human question: Why do good people suffer? The issue of theodicy is complex and troubling for many; both believers and nonbelievers wrestle with the challenge of understanding suffering in the face of a good and just God. The book of Job, however, provides no answer to this incredibly haunting question. Rather, Job wrestles with another fundamental question: What is the meaning of faith in the midst of suffering? From Job's exploration, we are led to consider this question for ourselves as we understand God through what we experience.

The book of Job is a complex mixture of prose and poetry in the larger body of the Hebrew Scriptures known as the wisdom books. Wisdom is not simply a framework for literature; it is a way of being in the world. The wise contemplate and explore the mysteries of life. The foundation of wisdom is the unequivocal belief that the world has order and purpose. The wise have the capacity to wait and see what the end will be with the assurance that whatever the outcome, God is still in control. Wisdom is exemplified in a popular saying in the African American church: "Thank God, troubles don't last always!" We encounter in the book of Job an excellent example of wisdom at work.

This book is primarily poetic—there is little prose. Because the book does not provide any historical data, we are not sure who wrote it or when. Most scholars concede that the book is more fictional than historical. The main characters are male; Job's first set of daughters are nameless and speechless. His second set of daughters are named by Job, and feminist scholars believe that Job's act of naming symbolizes a transformation for him personally and an act of rebellion against patriarchy that would have women nameless. His "new" daughters are beautiful, and Job grants each of them a share of the inheritance usually reserved for male children. Job's wife remains nameless and utters two sentences before she completely disappears. Despite Mrs. Job's brief appearance, her presence haunts the entire book.

We are introduced to Job immediately: "There was once a man in the land of Uz whose name was Job. That man was blameless and upright, one who feared God and turned away from evil" (Job 1:1).

Job is portrayed as a religious and moral person. Job is a really good person. The writer wants to leave no doubt about Job's character—he is the best of the best! The combination "blameless and upright" (Hebrew *tam* and *yashar*) implies completeness and perfection. Job is a person of meticulous integrity—his belief in God is complete, perfect, whole, wanting nothing.

Job has it all: a large family, livestock, servants, and status. He enjoys healthy and happy quality time with his three daughters and seven sons. He is the spiritual leader of his family: "When the feast days had run their course, Job would send and sanctify [his children], and he would rise early in the morning and offer burnt offerings according to the number of them all; for Job said, 'It may be that my children have sinned, and cursed God in their hearts.' This is what Job always did" (Job 1:5).

Just as Job's religious life is perfect, so is his family and social life. Note the inclusion of his daughters in the festivities; still, no mention has been made of Job's wife. Job is particularly concerned that no one in his family sins or curses God, even in the heart. Thus, he offers sacrifices on the family's behalf as well as his own.

The next scene provides the fodder for misunderstanding the book of Job. God is holding court in heaven. God's angels are reporting in and getting further instructions. One has the impression that this is a busy scene with lots of movement. The trouble starts for us with the entry of the *satan*. We equate the *satan* with the devil found later in Jewish and Christian works. Or we imagine the *satan* to be the embodiment of evil as seen in John Milton's *Paradise Lost*. Or we picture the Hollywood version of a being dressed in red with horns and a tail, waving a pitchfork. These are not the pictures the Hebrew is showing here.

The Hebrew word *hassatan* is not a proper noun; it is a generic term meaning "accuser" or "adversary" (see p. 347 of Carol A. Newsom reference in the Resources section). In Job, the *satan* is a member of God's divine assembly. The *satan*'s job is to ask questions and contest assumptions and the status quo. The *satan* is not God's equal and does not challenge God. Rather, the *satan* challenges God's assessments of human beings. The *satan* asks pointed questions. The exchange between God and the *satan* is rather simplistic:

God: My friend, where have you been?
The *satan*: Nowhere in particular; just cruising around, checking things out.
God: So, have you run across my main man, Job? You know, he's remarkable—he's got it all together. He loves me completely and totally. I wish all my people were as outstanding as he is.
The *satan*: Yeah, right! Why wouldn't he be totally devoted to you? He has nothing to complain about—every day is sunshine and roses for him. Things are just too easy for him!
God: What do you mean by that? I think Job is marvelous!
The *satan*: Of course you do. But I bet if Job experiences a cloudy day or a paper cut or a traffic jam, he'd . . .
God: Well, out with it. What do you think he'd do?
The *satan*: Aw, I just think we'd see a different side of him. If things got really rough for him, he might even curse you to your face!
God: Well, my friend, that sounds like a challenge.
The *satan*: Well, you know I am not a betting person, but I am sure that Job is not as great as you think.
God: All right, my friend! Let's just see about that. You can do anything to the stuff that Job has, but don't mess with his person. We will see what happens.
The *satan*: All righty, then. I'm out! See you later.

One day Job's world is turned upside down. A messenger brings distressing news: the oxen and donkeys have been lost to the invading Sabeans, who also killed the servants! Before Job can catch his breath from the shock, a second messenger arrives and interrupts the first: the sheep and some servants were struck by lightning and burned to death! Before this double whammy can sink in, a third messenger arrives and interrupts the second: the camels were stolen by the marauding Chaldeans, who also killed more servants! While he is still speaking, a fourth messenger arrives: a strong wind struck the eldest son's house; the house collapsed, and all the young people are dead!

Wow! Imagine the chaos of this scene. Imagine Job's shock—he has not had time to react and is probably numb and stunned to learn of all the losses. This is the test that God and the *satan* are holding their breaths over. Job's reaction will determine whether God is correct in God's initial assessment of Job's character. Job engages in the customary behavior in the face of catastrophe: "Then Job arose, tore his robe, shaved his head, and fell on the ground and worshiped" (Job 1:20).

He lifts up a prayer that may have been a traditional one; it is certainly poetic even today. He said, "Naked I came from my mother's womb, and naked shall I return there; God gave, and God has taken away; blessed be the name of God" (Job 1:21).

Job expresses the wisdom that the world still makes sense because God remains. Things are transient—here today and gone tomorrow. But God always is! Job does not get hung up on material things; they can always be replaced. The one constant is God—even when one's children die. Job knows that he came into this world with nothing and will leave this life with nothing. Everything is a gift from God. And God is free to take back gifts at any time. Job passes the test.

Later, God and the *satan* continue their conversation:

God: So, my friend, where have you been?
The *satan*: You know, my usual cruising.
God: Did you happen to run across my main man, Job? He still adores and worships me—despite all that you have done to him!
The *satan* Yeah! Yeah! Yeah! He has held on to his integrity. But you know, folks will willingly give up their things to protect themselves.
God: And just what is *that* supposed to mean?
The *satan*: I'm just saying, you know, that self-preservation is the rule of human life. Now, if you were to let me mess up his skin and bones—well, I believe he just might curse you to your face!
God: I don't think so! But let's just see about that. Do what you will, but don't kill him.
The *satan*: Okay! I will check in with you later.

The *satan* afflicts Job with sores from the bottom of his feet to the top of his head. These sores are unsightly and painful. They itch and ooze pus. Job seeks relief by scraping himself with broken pieces of pottery while he sits among the ashes. He seems to accept his new suffering as a continuation of the previous test. And now enters Mrs. Job—finally!

She confronts her husband with a question that she goes on to answer: "Do you still persist in your integrity? Curse God, and die" (Job 2:9).

These are the only words she speaks; and for them, she has been made into a symbol of faithlessness and evil. She is vilified as an uncaring, callous, and cold woman. Some commentators have tried to give a more sympathetic view of her, but we can explore her story without demeaning her. In this brief scene, she asks the absolute correct question. Her conclusion, however, is suspect.

Her story is similar to Mrs. Lot's in that it is difficult to unpack. We do not have a lot to go on. Yet Mrs. Job's speech gives us some straws at which to grasp. First, we have not encountered her in the earlier episodes concerning Job. We can only assume that she has participated in the joyous family times presented in the first chapter. We can surmise that she was grounded spiritually in God, as Job was. She may or may not have been present during Job's intercessory prayer and sacrifice times. Certainly, she was aware of his rituals and affirmed them as relevant and meaningful. So, when the disasters strike, she is affected. She, too, has lost everything. Neither she nor Job knows that their suffering is being allowed by God.

There are no explanations for their tragedies—they just happen. We cannot know for certain how Mrs. Job reacted to these catastrophes. Within patriarchy, her opinions and reactions are irrelevant. But what an incredible gift for us that she is allowed to speak: "Do you still persist in your integrity?"

This is the question to Job and to us. The popular belief of the day was that behavior dictated one's fortunes. Good people prospered; evil people did not. One did well because one did all the right things. One who did not prosper had failed in some way. When bad things happened, someone messed up.

The text does not specifically state this belief. But the exchange between God and the *satan* implies some understanding of this worldview. Therefore, when Job is tested, it is not because of anything that Job has done—his suffering is unmerited and undeserved. Job has remained blameless and upright. It is on this hinge that Mrs. Job enters the picture.

Indeed, it is easy to maintain integrity when things are going well. Now that disaster has struck, it may be necessary to reexamine one's wholesale belief in a just and merciful God. Mrs. Job encourages Job to consider his theological perspective. Losing things can be rationalized—you cannot take anything with you. So be it! But Job's person has been attacked. She tells Job to think about this. It is clear that Mrs. Job has evaluated the theology of her day—God is in control and has created good things. God has blessed them, so why, all of a sudden, have these bad things happened? Job needs to search himself.

Job's integrity is symbolic of one whose life is transparent—what you see is what you get. And what you get are total honesty about life and total devotion to God. If Job is truly blameless and upright, he will remain steadfast no matter what. Death, then, becomes almost anticlimactic—maintaining one's faith while under attack is the ultimate goal. Death has no power over the truly righteous; if they have given their very life over to God, nothing can hurt them.

There is nothing evil or wrong about posing the question. If Job has any doubt about the goodness of God, he should voice it, own up to it, and suffer (pun intended!) the consequences. A person of integrity can do no less. Mrs. Job's question challenges Job to be clear about his position and his faith: Is he going to hold on to God despite his present difficulties, or is he going to give up, give out, give in to his anger and grief? It is a question that we all confront in crises. The way in which we choose to handle our catastrophes says volumes about who we are and what we truly believe. In times of trouble, we discover who God is for us and who we are in God. Real belief means that our experiences are to be taken seriously—we are not detached from the things that happen to us. To be fully human is to interact fully with all that surrounds us.

Mrs. Job's question pushes Job to determine whether he has given lip service to having integrity or whether the core of his being is about integrity. In other words, Mrs. Job asks, do you *do* integrity or *are* you integrity? The question is astonishing; that patriarchy would let her pose it is even more astonishing. This question probes the depths of the mystery of faith. It is the kind of question that God would ask. Indeed, God is constantly asking Israel where its heart, the center of its being, really is. Israel, at times in its history, has given only superficial homage to integrity. In good times, Israel has played at religion and faithfulness. The times of prosperity made the nation lazy and complacent. However, crises have a way of making one's core evident. In tough times, Israel has given in to the emotions of despair, fear, resignation, and anger. In times of deep tragedy, Israel has called upon God for help. Have you ever noticed how fervent and earnest your prayers are in times of crisis and danger?

In good times, our prayers may become soft and surface. When the shadows come, we get "real" in our conversations with God. Many of the psalms reflect the earnest prayers of one teetering on the cliff of destruction. Mrs. Job, with a stroke of genius, poses the question of the ages: Do you still persist in your integrity?

In this question, she affirms God's evaluation of Job—he is blameless and upright. He fears God and turns away from evil. If in the face of unexplained and unexplainable suffering, one can still revere and honor God, that one has integrity. There is a marked similarity between Job and Abraham in this sense. If Abraham had refused to sacrifice Isaac, God's authority would have been undermined. Abraham's willingness to destroy what meant the most to him showed that his ultimate concern was God, not Isaac. We may be a little disheartened at this; many of us say that God is the most important thing in our lives. But some of us are not being honest. We place other people and other things before God. Our children, our spouses or partners, our parents are more important. For some of us, status symbols—education, careers, wealth, material things—are more important. For still others, social status—power, influence, control—is more important.

Mrs. Job's question haunts us as we try to make our way in the world. If her question affirms God's assessment of Job, her response affirms that of the *satan*. The *satan* has challenged God's glowing pride in Job. The *satan* believes that human beings are devoted to God only because it is to their advantage to do so. For these people, God is a cosmic bellhop to be manipulated into doing the human beings' bidding. God is not the creator of heavens and earth and the fullness therein. God is not the rock and refuge in times of trouble. God is not the good shepherd who shelters them in the shadows of the valley. God is cool as long as folks get what they want. But when God is slow in dispensing blessings, these people move on to the next god!

Having asked a profound question, Mrs. Job looks at her husband and despairs. He is already as good as dead. What hope is there for him? How can he recover from all this? He should just cut his losses, fold his hand, and give in to death. This is the response the *satan* anticipates and predicts. Human beings do not love God because God is the Divine. They love God for what God can and will do for them. They will forsake God as soon as the good times stop.

But Job reacts to her advice: "'You speak as any foolish woman would speak. Shall we receive the good at the hand of God, and not receive the bad?' In all this Job did not sin with his lips" (Job 2:10). He cuts her down to size—her speech is like that of a foolish person. By this, Job is saying her conclusion is the opposite of wisdom. He acknowledges her right to an opinion and does not attack her as a person. Her words, though, are incorrect. We cannot be sure whether Mrs. Job cursed God or whether she wanted to. She is setting out an alternative choice for Job, who wholeheartedly rejects it, at least at this point. Job is the focus. Mrs. Job's thoughts are not deemed relevant.

However, her probing question summarizes and embodies the challenge between God and the *satan*—she makes clear to Job and to us the real issue. When tragedy and disaster strike us, we are likely to moan and cry out, "Why me? What did I do to deserve this?" We are fervent in our pleas because we are trying to make sense of what has happened. We assume that there is some kind of order, some kind of justice in the created order that will protect us from capricious evil. We want life to be fair. If we do what we are supposed to do, then things will go well for and with us. If we sin and are aware of it, then we can handle the consequences because we know we deserve to suffer. But we are disoriented and thrown for a loop when bad things happen by chance. We want to believe that things happen for a reason. We want to understand why things happen. We refuse to believe that things just happen or that things can really be chalked up to accident. We want to blame someone or something in order to let ourselves off the hook. We do not want to look at ourselves—we may not like what we find. We want to pretend that we are attuned to God's will and that we are under God's just and protective care.

Mrs. Job taps in to these very human emotions and fears. She tells us that the question is not, "Why me?" It is, "Why not me? What do I do in the middle of this crisis?" Although he dismisses her response, Job will ponder her question throughout the rest of the book. For now, he holds on to his integrity by posing an alternative response to Mrs. Job's question. He holds on because he truly believes that everything—good and bad—is in God's control. By his speech in Job 2:10, he has one-upped her. He is more mature in his faith. She reacts to the moment as if life is a series of unrelated episodes. He reacts as if life is a drama and the present moment is just one act in a multiact play.

Within patriarchy, he has shut her up! At this point he is morally and religiously superior to her. Mrs. Job then disappears, and we never hear of her again. In the end, Job's family is restored—three daughters and seven sons. His wealth and status are restored. Yet as in the beginning, there is no mention of his wife.

Job passes the second test. After his conversation with his wife, Job is visited by three friends, Eliphaz, Bildad, and Zophar. They pay a pastoral call on their dear friend. For seven days, they sit in silence. When Job speaks, his tone is markedly different. He is no longer the calm, suffering, saintly man of faith. His tone echoes that of Mrs. Job—he does not curse God, but he rues the day he was born and wishes he had never been born. (Read Job 3:11, 16–17, 20–22, 25–26.)

Job does not wish to die, but he expresses the anguish of his present life. If he had never been born, he would not be so miserable as he is now. Job is in the depths of despair, and he articulates his feelings in the most pitiful terms imaginable. He is in pain, the deepest pain of his existence, and needs a word to reassure him that God is still with him. Job totters on the brink of faith and faithlessness, hope and hopelessness, life and death.

Perhaps Job spent the seven days after his talk with Mrs. Job meditating on her question and searching his heart. She was right, after all! The rest of the book chronicles Job's friends' attempt to console him. In essence, they offer the same solution as Mrs. Job—admit that you have sinned and deserve what has happened to you. Job does not budge and eventually engages God in a conversation.

Job's confrontation with God is a mixed bag of emotions. On the one hand, Job has serious doubts about God's power and authority. On the other hand, he does not wish to totally abandon his trust and belief in a good God. To do so would leave Job vulnerable to death. God's challenge to Job confirms that Mrs. Job was on the right track to seeking truth.

The question is not, "Why do the righteous suffer?" Rather, it is, "How is the believer to respond in the face of adversity?" Job and his friends ponder and debate the question. Job wants an explanation from God concerning the condition of the world. Job dares to question God's motives and power and concern. After much agony, Job is able to resolve his question. The bottom line for Job is that God is trustworthy, in good times and bad, in joy and sorrow.

After a thorough cataloging of God's deeds on behalf of the created order, Job realizes that he will never fully understand the mysteries of faith. But his experiences of tragedy and disaster and his own survival of them have opened a new dimension of knowing and faith for him. He now knows something he did not know before: God has not promised us blue skies and sunshine. God has not promised an easy, painless way. God has not promised us wealth and fame. God has not promised us the good life. Instead, and remarkably so, God has promised God's very presence through all of life. Whatever our experience, we have the assurance that we do not suffer alone. For those who are oppressed, whether the oppression is racism, sexism, ageism, militarism, colonialism, domestic violence, or homophobia, God is with them. We are not to be passive in the face of oppression and discrimination. We are encouraged and challenged to work against the powers of evil—with all our might and with all the resources at our disposal. But when it is all said and done, our hope is not in our efforts. Our hope is in God's willingness to love us in our pain and to deliver or sustain us.

Mrs. Job asks the right question. Our hope is that, given time to reflect on her experience of pain and her survival of it, she would have voiced what Job came to learn:

> Then Job answered God:
> "I know that you can do all things,
> and that no purpose of yours can be thwarted.
> 'Who is this that hides counsel without knowledge?'
> Therefore I have uttered what I did not understand,
> things too wonderful for me, which I did not know.

'Hear, and I will speak;
I will question you, and you declare to me.'
I had heard of you by the hearing of the ear,
but now my eye sees you;
therefore I despise myself,
and repent in dust and ashes." (Job 42:1–6)

Mrs. Job was not a cold, uncaring, faithless woman. She was a woman who understood suffering and pain. She was a woman who thought about her situation and tried to see the options available to her. She was a woman who pushes us to think about who we are and whose we are—really. Thank God that Mrs. Job was brave enough to speak out and speak up!

REFLECTION QUESTIONS

1. Have you ever been made to feel that your opinion did not matter? What did you do in response?
2. What can be done to encourage more women to speak out on matters of oppression and discrimination?
3. What are some obstacles that prevent oppressed persons from working together?
4. Mrs. Job clearly is an outsider in the theological debate with Job. Yet she rightly critiques the fundamental assumptions of that debate. What criticism do you offer of Christianity?
5. What is your image of God? What images of God are depicted in the opening chapters of Job?
6. How do you define "evil"?
7. God does not cause Job's misery, but allows it. What are the implications for how we understand evil, undeserved suffering, and oppression?
8. The *satan* is a member of God's heavenly council. How does this change your understanding of evil? Of the devil?
9. How do you deal with adversity? What lessons have you learned from this story?
10. Mrs. Job's appearance is brief, but she makes a major impact. What are the implications for women's use of power?
11. Both feminist and womanist theology start with the experiences of women and black women as the basis for understanding God. How have your experiences shaped your faith?
12. How can you use your personal experiences to help others?

9

GOMER: VIXEN OR VICTIM?

The story of Gomer is one I wish had not been written. The book of Hosea is very difficult to decipher and understand. The way Gomer is depicted is extremely painful. The image of God as a long-suffering husband who abuses his wife into submission places women in a dilemma when they try to study this book and to find inspiration in it. The text presents insurmountable interpretative problems; much of the time, scholars can only guess about meaning and context. It would be easier to avoid Gomer and Hosea altogether. And I was tempted!

The research I conducted left my head spinning and my emotions twirling. I was just as confused when I actually read the text. Hosea is a hard book to read and study. And Gomer leaves me wanting to rescue her from Hosea and the patriarchical society that permitted her abuse. Gomer does not utter one word. Speeches assigned to her are voiced by her husband, who may or may not have quoted her accurately or quoted her at all—these words may be wishful thinking on his part. I warn you that our time with Gomer will be painful. But there are important lessons for us if we at least attempt to hear her story.

Hosea was a prophet who worked in Israel, the Northern Kingdom. He preached from the end of Jeroboam II's reign to just before Israel's capture by the Assyrians. Hosea appeared on the scene two kings after King Jehu, who assassinated Jezebel. Jehu's mission was to rid Israel of Baal worship. Under Jeroboam II's administration, Israel prospered—cities were conquered, taxation produced great wealth, and the people flourished. On the heels of prosperity, however, came social and religious decline. Kings were assassinated, a bitter war was fought with Syria, bad political alliances were made, and there was a resurgence of Baal worship. Israel was never completely purged of Baalism, and its cults coexisted with God throughout the land with little opposition. The task of the prophet in those days was to hold the people accountable to God's covenant. Hosea had his work cut out for him.

The belief was that as long as Israel kept God's covenant, things would go well. Israel's political and economic woes were opportunities to reconsider God's covenant, to repent, and to renew the faith that the nation experienced in its earliest history.

Israel had long sought relevant and meaningful ways to talk about God. The attempts could not hide the limitations of language. Unable to articulate the essence of God, Israel used symbols to talk about God. These images vary according to the tradition at the time. In some ways, God is like a potter fashioning human beings from the dust and dirt. In other ways, God is like a clothier stitching fine garments from animal skins. In still other ways, God is like a fertility specialist opening closed wombs of barren women. God is like a warrior-ruler fighting Israel's battles. God is like a structural engineer making a road through the Sea of Reeds (Red Sea). God is a divine nutritionist sending manna from the wilderness skies and giving water from stones. In the attempts to say what God is like, Israel used the images of light, refuge, wind, breath. God is not these things, of course. But the comparisons attempt to get at what God is like. God is more than all these things and much, much more.

Hosea meditates on the history of God's people and is struck by the utter patience of a caring God who forgives and embraces time and time again. Hosea understands that something unexplainable is happening that previous images do not convey. The people do whatever they want, and still God chooses to be in relationship with them. God is steadfast and constant; the people are fickle and ambivalent. How can Hosea talk about this phenomenon in terms that the people will understand? He uses a new image—the relationship between God and Israel is like that of a husband and an adulterous wife.

Hosea is the first to use the image of marriage as a metaphor for understanding the divine–human relationship. Hosea poses God as the faithful husband and Israel as the wayward wife. As long as we remember that this image is a *metaphor*, we are fine. What has happened, though, is that interpreters have moved the image from what points to something about relationships to a norm. God is male, the thinking goes, and superior. Women are inferior and deserve to be treated as such. Therefore, men have the right to abuse women to keep them under control.

For women in ancient Israel, marriage had little to do with love. As we learned earlier, marriage as an institution was not especially liberating for women. Women were expected to be monogamous, while men could have many wives and concubines. A woman married into her husband's family and moved into his father's house. Marriages were usually arranged by the male of the family; women were seldom given a choice of whether or not to marry a particular man. Adultery was a big sin with harsh penalties for both the man and the woman. The punishment was rarely carried out, however. Adulterous women were in greater danger of being punished. The marriage contract carried obligations for both partners. Marriage was not designed to be an equal partnership. Women were dependent upon their husbands. The rare woman who was independent, bold, assertive is the exception. She would be considered dangerous—someone to fear and thus someone to destroy.

Coupled with the privilege of marriage was the man's concern for his honor. A man's honor conveyed his status and place within the culture. A man who managed to provide a good life for himself and his family was an honorable man. As long as he carried himself well, his honor remained intact. If tragedy struck, his honor was questioned (remember Job!). A man's honor was tied up with his ability to provide for his family and his ability to control his wife. A husband could be shamed by the behavior of the women in his house; wives, daughters, granddaughters, and unmarried sisters were all under his control. Women's sexuality (sexual behavior, ability to bear children, body functions) was subject to men's control; women who misbehaved brought dishonor upon the men who controlled them.

Hosea probably chose the marriage image precisely because it highlighted the gap in the power dynamic. God loves Israel as a man loves an adulterous wife. God is the superior one in the relationship. God chooses God's mate and expects total dependence and loyalty. God sets the rules and expects the mate to keep them. The demands and rules are set to protect both parties—they are not just whimsical demands. The husband has the responsibility to shelter, clothe, feed, protect, and provide material comforts for his wife. In exchange for these privileges, the wife gives her husband control of her sexuality and her loyalty.

When the mate fails to keep the rules of the marriage, God has the choice to keep the mate or reject her. In a patriarchal sense, the disobedient wife makes her husband a victim. She jeopardizes his well-being in the culture, and he must decide what to do about his victimization. Time and time again, Hosea notices, God forgives. God sends the wayward wife away, but soon searches for her to restore the broken relationship. God goes to great lengths to keep the marriage together.

Hosea's audience is all men. There are no women present. In an effort to shock his audience into a new hearing of his message, Hosea uses an image they could relate to personally, something they have experienced. Not all the men would be the victims of adulterous wives, but they would know the danger of such an occurrence. If a man could forgive and continue to live with a wife who had brought shame upon him, then maybe Israelite men could understand how God loves them. The wayward wife (Israel) is loved by a mate (God) who deserves better, yet wants the wife! Remember that Hosea is using a metaphor to shock his audience. They need to hear—really hear—what God is trying to say.

Hosea's use of female sexuality is difficult to hear. The lengths to which the faithful husband will go to retrieve his wife are violent. The symbol of woman as promiscuous is unfair. But as a metaphor, the image is effective. God is the faithful husband married to a woman (Israel) who goes after other lovers (gods, Baal). Because Hosea 1–3 develops the marriage image, we will focus our study on these chapters.

God and Hosea want to grab Israel's attention and show the nation something it has never seen before. No man in his right mind would knowingly marry a woman who sleeps with other men and has children with her lovers. Nothing would have startled Hosea's audience more. No doubt, some of the men would rather die than marry such a woman.

Commentators have wrestled with exactly what kind of woman Hosea is asked to marry. Some translations state that Hosea is to marry a "harlot." Others state that she is a "prostitute." The New Revised Standard Version renders the term "whore." The woman is not technically a prostitute. She is like a harlot in that she has many partners. Her activity is a series of adulteries; she is promiscuous. She seeks and goes after other lovers. Israel, likewise, seeks and goes after other gods (remember the issue of Baal worship in the Jezebel story).

Marrying a promiscuous woman would make Hosea's audience sit up and take notice. Hosea follows God's command. We do not know much about Gomer other than her name. We do not know if Diblaim refers to her birthplace or her father's name. She is a woman without family or home. She is an outcast; her reputation is well known. Otherwise, how does Hosea know to choose her? As a promiscuous woman, she is "damaged goods." No man would want to marry or stay married to her because she cannot be trusted. She has jeopardized her future by making herself unmarriageable. That Hosea marries her is quite shocking.

The plot continues. Hosea and Gomer marry and start a family. (Read Hosea 1:3–8.)

The names of the three children born to Gomer and Hosea symbolize the condition of Israel:

➤ The elder son, Jezreel, symbolizes the site of Ahab and Jezebel's royal home. You will remember that it was in Jezreel that King Jehu assassinated Jezebel as a final act of eliminating Baalism from Israel. She shamed him by comparing him to Zimri, who killed his master. According to Hosea, Jehu's family is to be punished for the bloodbath, and the punishment extends to the entire house (kingdom) of Israel; this is a foreshadowing of the exile to come.

➤ The second child is a daughter, Lo-ruhamah, who symbolizes God's disconnection from the Northern Kingdom (Israel); God will have continued compassion for Judah. But God has no feelings for Israel.

➤ The youngest child is a son named Lo-ammi, who symbolizes the severed covenantal relationship between God and Israel. God has given up on Israel.

The names of the children have been used to show the devastating consequences of Israel's unfaithfulness. In Israel, communion with God and connectedness to God's people were everything. To be cast out or cut off was to be homeless, an exile—the ultimate in despair. To be disconnected was worse than death. If God makes the covenant null and void, the people are truly hopeless.

Yet in the face of utter destruction, there is the possibility of hope. In the next chapter, the names of the two younger children have been changed to indicate that the indictment upon Israel has been withdrawn: Lo-ammi is now Ammi; Lo-ruhamah is now Ruhamah. The children are urged to take a message to their mom—maybe they can help her come to her senses before it is too late:

> Or I will strip her naked
> and expose her as in the day she was born,
> and make her like a wilderness,
> and turn her into a parched land,
> and kill her with thirst. (Hos. 2:3)

Hosea gives her an ultimatum: return home, change her wicked ways, or he will be forced to take drastic measures. Gomer has another chance to make things right. But she has to give up her wayward behavior. Likewise, Israel has another chance. If Israel stops chasing other gods, God will restore the relationship. God is calling for total and complete devotion. There is no room for ambivalence. God has tired of Israel's wishy-washy ways. God demands a decision from Israel.

If Gomer chooses to continue in her promiscuity, she has pushed Hosea to the edge. He has to fight back. She has left him no choice. She deserves the public humiliation and violence he will inflict. The punishment is harsh and extreme. It is humiliating and degrading. As we learned earlier, punishment for adultery is stoning to death. But what Hosea proposes is over the top! Hosea, though, has a legitimate complaint. His wife has moved way beyond the limits of Israelite tolerance. Her actions have been extreme, and his actions must match hers if he is to maintain a sense of honor and dignity.

Likewise, Israel has shamed its God. Israel has gone time and time again after Baal; the nation has learned nothing. Israel acts worse now than it did before God chose the nation and made it a people. After all that God has done for this people, how can they continue in their wicked ways? Israel merits no mercy. The nation gets what it deserves—total and complete humiliation in the form of defeat and exile.

The children are placed in an unfortunate situation—in the middle of their parents' mess! They are told to appeal to their mom to stop her wicked ways. If she does not, things will not go well for her.

Hosea states his case passionately. Gomer goes to her lovers for the needs that Hosea should be fulfilling. Because she looks for love in all the wrong places, Hosea will keep her away from her lovers by putting up barriers. She will seek her lovers, but she will not be able to find them. She will learn in due time that what she needs is only what Hosea, her legal husband, can provide. She is to be totally dependent on him whether she likes it or not. (Read Hosea 2:7.)

To show Gomer how dependent she is on him and how good he has been to her, Hosea will withdraw his support; he will expose her shame; he will put an end to her parties; and he will punish her for having a good time with her lovers:

> Now I will uncover her shame
> in the sight of her lovers,
> and no one shall rescue her out of my hand. (Hos. 2:10)

After publicly humiliating and abusing her both emotionally and physically, Hosea will seduce her. He hopes she will be repentant and grateful. He hopes they will forge ahead with their relationship. He will reclaim her, and she will renounce her lovers. He will make her forget her lovers altogether; it will be as if she had never strayed. As a sign of their recommitment, Hosea will claim Gomer's children as his own, and all will be right again.

Likewise, Israel has been looking for love in all the wrong places. By allowing Israel to live with the consequences of its choice to be with Baal and other gods, God permits the nation to flounder and sink into total depravity. By God's withdrawal of divine justice, compassion, care, and protection, Israel is left to see just how beneficent the Canaanite gods are and will be. God is convinced that the Israelites will be nothing without the God who brought them out of slavery in Egypt as "nobodies" through the wilderness to a place where they are "somebodies"! Once they experience life without the one true God, they will gladly reunite with God. Once they find themselves in the wilderness again, God will show them what they have missed by not committing themselves wholly to God. Once they taste God's goodness, they will repent and make a real, binding commitment. All will be restored, and the punishments and abuse will be forgotten. (See Hos. 2:14–23.)

Hosea 3 is a complex five-verse chapter. The prophet receives another command from God concerning an adulterous woman. It is not clear whether this chapter is a continuation of Hosea 1 or a completely different incident. Further, it is not clear whether this woman in Hosea 3 is Gomer or a different woman. Also, it is unclear why Hosea has to buy her. In Hosea 1, there was a question about Gomer's character; here there is a question about Hosea's feelings. In Hosea 1, the prophet is told to "take for/to himself" a wife; here in Hosea 3, he is told to "love/show love for" an adulterous woman.

As we have seen in Rebekah's and Delilah's stories, women do not fare well when men "love" them. Women in ancient Israel would probably not understand our modern notions about love and marriage. For many of them, love meant having their basic human and economic needs met. Romance and passion were not integral parts of the marriage contract. So, when we learn that Hosea is to love an adulterous woman, we are intrigued. He purchases her with silver and stuff of the earth: grain and wine. Then he says a curious thing to her: "You must remain as mine for many days; you shall not play the whore, you shall not have intercourse with a man, nor I with you" (Hos. 3:3).

Though he loves her, they are not to consummate their relationship. Hosea tries to make sure that she has changed her wayward behavior. The sexless period parallels Israel's period of exile. The nation will have no form of government or religion or economy. Their destitute state will be the spark to their repentance and restoration as God's people.

And so, we have the complicated and difficult story of Gomer. This confusing and terrifying story is uncomfortable for modern women and men to study. It is important to remember a few things.

First, this story was intended for men. It is a story by a man, for men. The prophet Hosea needed a way to help his people understand their condition of social and political decline. Their troubles stemmed from their faulty, inadequate religious life. If they could get their understandings of God clear, the other aspects of their lives would fall into place.

Many people believe that our problems of poverty, crime, discrimination, and injustice, among others, stem from our faulty spirituality. If believers behaved and functioned as the people of God, our social problems would be solved. If we believed that we are created in the image and likeness of God, we would value human life and not resort to the exploitation that creates hunger and homelessness for many around the world. If we believed that we are part of God's plan for creation, we would not impose our insecurities on others through war, discrimination, or violence. The notion that social ills are rooted in theological ills is not new.

Instead of seeing the joy of serving the living God, Israel continued seeking the blessings of other gods. Their trials, troubles, and tribulations only highlighted the foolishness and uselessness of seeking other gods. God alone is sufficient. Failure to realize this truth made Israel vulnerable to the whims of fate. The best way to convey this message is through the image of the faithful husband and the adulterous wife.

Second, this story tries to make concrete an abstract concept. Hosea wants the men of Israel to know clearly how much God wants to be in an intimate relationship with them. God is patient, long-suffering, and forgiving. Hosea exaggerates the marital relationship to shock his audience. Only in the extreme can this group of men get a glimpse of what it is like being in a relationship with God. God loves God's wayward people and will do anything, including humiliating and abusing them, to bring them back into relationship. God's actions hurt God more than they hurt the people. But God is willing to endure the pain if, in the end, the people return ready for a new and fresh start. In other words, the ends justify the means if God is reunited with God's beloved people.

Third, the marriage contract in ancient Israel differed greatly from that of today. Marriage partners were not equal. The man was superior in every way to the woman. Though the man was in charge, both partners had responsibilities and were obligated to perform their duties. The double standard let men off the hook, for their future would remain secure. The women carried the burden of breaking the marriage vows by their behavior. Because a woman could bring shame and dishonor on her man, she had to be controlled and held to a higher standard. Today, many of us are appalled by such thinking. In large segments of the world, however, the patriarchal view of marriage prevails.

Finally, the image of God as faithful husband married to a promiscuous wife is a metaphor. It is, by its nature, figurative rather than literal. It is important to understand the *spirit and intention* of the image—to convey to a hard-headed, unthinking group of men the mysteries of faith in a loving, caring, and forgiving God. Hosea uses the marriage metaphor to make concrete something that is elusive and unexplainable. Hosea's audience would have heard this metaphor because it tapped into patriarchal understandings of ancient Israel: that God is distinctly male; that husbands must maintain control of women's sexuality; that violence toward women is a viable means of control; that in cases of adultery, the husband is the victim because his property and reputation are at stake.

We have been warned not to impose twentieth-century understandings on the ancient texts of the Bible. Gomer's story certainly stands as a witness to this warning. Gomer never speaks, and we have no sense of who she is or what motivates her. We do not know who her family is. We do not know how she becomes involved in promiscuity. We do not know what she sees as alternatives or options. All we know is that she is married and the mother of three children, including a daughter. Her husband has rejected her children. She is a victim of domestic and sexual abuse. We see her as a pitiful creature without voice and without power. Gomer is part of a metaphor that tells us how wonderful a faithful husband is, at her expense. Our inability to focus fully on Gomer is due to the major role that Hosea assigns to God. Gomer is like a ghost haunting her own story! Her presence is eerie and elusive. We never get to meet her, and Hosea's words about her are degrading, controlling, and unflattering.

Gomer is a woman who cannot be faithful, but we never know why. We never see her interacting with her husband, her lovers, or her children. We have no clue about her thoughts and feelings. She raises more questions for us: Was she looking for love or addicted to sex? Did she commit adultery as a rebellious act against patriarchal limits on women? How did she feel about herself? After Hosea's abuse, why did she return to him?

In the midst of so many probing questions, Gomer remains silent. How different she seems from Mrs. Potiphar and Mrs. Job. How different she seems from Jezebel and Delilah. Her presence makes a point for men and leaves women with unanswerable questions.

We want something more, something better for Gomer. We want her to have a mind and a voice. We want her to be bold and to fight back against her abusive husband. We want her to speak to us about hope and possibility. We want her to be good, strong, and proud. Hosea has not given us such a woman. And at the end of her story, we are left to pray: heaven help us all!

REFLECTION QUESTIONS

1. What disturbs you most about Gomer's story?
2. The marriage metaphor affirms that Israel sees itself in a relationship with God. What other metaphors of this relationship have we seen? Which are most relevant for modern believers?
3. In this story, God is one who loves and punishes; banishes and seduces; humiliates and restores. How do these images shape your understanding of God?
4. What are your notions about marriage? What are the responsibilities of each partner? Be specific.
5. Is the marriage metaphor relevant to modern believers? Who would find the image affirming? Who would find it offensive?
6. What advice would you give Gomer about her life? Be specific.
7. What should we do with biblical stories and teachings that seem old-fashioned and oppressive?
8. What can be done to eliminate domestic, sexual, and child abuse?
9. Why do people stay in abusive, unhealthy relationships?
10. What would happen to Hosea's metaphor if God were the adulterous wife? Have a good time imagining this.
11. What is the place of forgiveness in relationships marked by violence and abuse?
12. How can you forgive and forget?

10

HERODIAS: HEARTLESS OR HURT?

$\mathcal{T}$he story of Herodias introduces us to women of the Christian Scriptures (New Testament). Just as we saw in the Hebrew Scriptures, the lives of women receive very little attention. We find women continuing the roles assigned to them and as evidenced in the Hebrew Scriptures. Women continue to create homes, work fields, care for others. In addition, in the Christian Scriptures, we find women with active spiritual and prayer lives. Further, we find women of considerable wealth who make major contributions to the work of Jesus and Paul. We find strong women who speak and take risks.

However, women still suffered under patriarchal notions about the place of women. So, again, many women are unnamed. A few women wielded political power, but they were the exceptions. The masses of women continued the work their mamas and grandmamas and great-grandmamas did. The major difference in the Christian Scriptures is the way Jesus interacted with women. Jesus defied patriarchal custom and treated women with respect and honor. He counted among his disciples and friends women of substance. Although the general plight of women was not changed, their connection with Jesus made a difference in how they saw the world and the opportunities available to them.

The Gospel writers included women in Jesus' genealogy, and women played a major role in the ministry and work of Jesus. He did not exclude women, and he regarded them as equals to men. The first Christian evangelists and preachers were women who testified about how things had changed because of Jesus of Nazareth. When the male disciples fled after Jesus' crucifixion, the women remained. When the male disciples were hiding in the upper room after Jesus' burial, the women were at the tomb. When Jesus appeared after the resurrection, the women were there. Jesus commanded the women to go and tell the men—women were the first Christian preachers!

Jesus ushered in a new way of relating to women, but the larger society continued its patriarchal ways. It is not surprising, then, that we find several "bad girls" in the Christian Scriptures. Their "crimes" mirror the crimes of our sisters in the Hebrew Scriptures—misuse of power and adultery, for example—and they serve as metaphors or lessons for men.

One of the bad girls is Herodias, whose story is found in Matthew and Mark. We first will look at Mark's version of her story and compare it to Matthew's version.

Just as I did in examining the Hebrew Scriptures, I will spend a little time providing background information that may help us understand the women we will be studying. The overall theological purpose of the "author" will convey some sense of how women's stories figure into their wider interests. We encounter the same difficulties in the Christian Scriptures as in the Hebrew Scriptures—we cannot be certain about the author of any particular work. We know that the works of the Christian Scriptures are compilations of oral and written traditions that were formalized some time after the actual events.

We find some continuation of Israelite thought patterns and perspectives into the new era after the Exile. The people believed that the devastation of being conquered and scattered by bigger powers was the consequence of their faithlessness to God. Because they did not keep God's covenant, they were duly punished. They expected to be fully restored as a world power after a time of exile and oppression. The first century, however, found them still waiting. There was a continuing need to explain their plight, so many of the social and religious constructs from the D tradition were operative: the one true God had chosen the Israelites and established a covenantal relationship with them; the covenant relationship required their total love, trust, worship, and service to God, and in return, God would provide blessings or curses depending on Israel's fulfillment of the covenant; and the role of women was still subordinate to men.

An important difference for the new generation of Israelites was a growing body of official religious texts. The sacred literature consisted mostly of Deuteronomy, the historical books (First and Second Samuel and First and Second Kings), wisdom literature (Psalms), and works of the prophets. The nation had a literature it could refer to and teach to future generations. It is not clear how definitive and comprehensive the body of literature was, but it indicated that Israel had a history and a legacy equal to those of other world powers.

Most scholars believe that Mark is the earliest of the Gospels to be written and that both Matthew and Luke used Mark's work as a basis for their own. Further, scholars believe that a collection of sayings by Jesus called Q circulated and was included in the first three Gospels, which are called the Synoptics (Matthew, Mark, and Luke). Each of the Synoptic Gospels provides a similar view of Jesus and uses much of the same material. Each Gospel has an overall theological perspective that determines how materials are redacted.

Commentators believe that Mark's Gospel reflects an early Christian urban setting dominated by Roman power and influence; they also believe that the audience was composed of non-Jewish or Gentile believers. Mark takes great pains to explain Hebrew words and customs. City life would have been difficult for newcomers who had to work hard and were subject to disease and isolation. In many ways, Mark's context foreshadows modern cities—overcrowding; inadequate housing, employment, and medical resources; the search for meaning. The messages of John the Baptist and Jesus of Nazareth would hold great appeal for the masses of people.

The story of Herodias is part of John the Baptist's story. John the Baptist is first introduced in Mark 1:4. John appears in the wilderness preaching and baptizing people from miles around. John's message is one of repentance and preparation for a new thing God is doing. He stands in the tradition of prophets of the Hebrew Scriptures and prepares the way for the ministry of Jesus. In Mark 1:14, we learn that John has been arrested, but we are not told why. We find out in Mark 6.

The account of John the Baptist's death follows Jesus' visit to his home in Nazareth. Jesus is teaching on the Sabbath in the synagogue. The people are amazed at his teachings, especially since he is their hometown boy. Their disbelief, however, prevents Jesus from continuing his teaching and healing. He leaves there to work among the area villages. He commissions his disciples to go in pairs to teach and heal. Their ministries are successful, and word of their endeavors reaches Herod, the Roman governor of Galilee and Perea. Herod confesses that he beheaded John and Jesus seems to be a reincarnation of John.

The details of John's demise are recorded in a flashback: Herod arrests John in order to keep his wife, Herodias, from having John assassinated. John functions as a prophet and criticizes Herod and Herodias for marrying each other. John the Baptist publicly condemns Herod Antipas for divorcing his first wife to marry Herodias, who divorced her husband, Herod Philip, who was also Herod Antipas's brother. John speaks out against this based on Israelite law and custom. The *levir,* or duty of a husband's brother, outlined in Deuteronomy 25:5–10 applies only if the brother is dead. John's troubles with the Herodian court are similar to those of Elijah with Ahab and Jezebel.

The royal family does not like John's airing of the royal dirty laundry in public, and we are told that Herodias "had a grudge against him, and wanted to kill him. But she could not" (Mark 6:19). The Greek word translated "grudge" is from a root meaning to "hold on or over," "strive after," or "entangle oneself with." Herodias does not simply dislike John's statements—she has it in for him. She will go to any length to shut him up. Her problem is that she does not have the power to kill him. Her husband does (remember Potiphar's wife and Joseph?). However, her husband is afraid to kill him because Herod fears John. He knows John is "righteous and holy." The Greek words (*dikaios* and *hagios*) imply that John is innocent, blameless, with a character of impeccable integrity. Herod is in awe of John. And so he protects John from the death Herodias wishes for him. Herod is puzzled by John's message but likes to listen to him. John is a charismatic figure who generates admiration and loyalty. It would be a risky political move to have John killed. The royal family is already on shaky ground because of its immoral family situation. Herod does not want to add to the family's troubles with credibility. As far as John the Baptist is concerned, Herod and Herodias have committed incest, which is an abomination. And they have brought shame upon an already shameful family.

Herodias is not able to kill John, but she does not forget him. An opportunity will soon present itself. The occasion is Herod's birthday party. He has invited all the really important folks from Galilee to the grand event: "When his daughter Herodias came in and danced, she pleased Herod and his guests; and the king said to the girl, 'Ask me for whatever you wish, and I will give it.' And he solemnly swore to her, 'Whatever you ask me, I will give you, even half of my kingdom'" (Mark 6:22–23).

The text does not clarify the identity of the young dancer. Most scholars state that she is Herodias's daughter from her first marriage. Although the text does not indicate, she is popularly thought to be Salome. At any rate, she dances for Herod, who is moved to make a startling proposition. Some scholars assert that it would have been improper for a daughter of the household to dance on such an occasion. The royal families did not display themselves in that way. Others see a suggestion that the dance was lewd or sexual. The text does not state what kind of dance she performed or why it moved Herod. This is a party, after all, and there are likely wine and strong drink. Herod's family history indicates great dysfunction, so anything is likely to have happened.

On a whim, he promises her anything she wants. He probably thinks she will ask for money or land—something to secure her financial or material future. But the young girl seeks her mother's advice, and her mother sees an opportunity to do away with John the Baptist. Herodias does not seem content that John is in prison; only his death will satisfy her. "She went out and said to her mother, 'What should I ask for?' She replied, 'The head of John the baptizer'" (Mark 6:24).

Herod is distressed at her request. But he has promised her in front of all his friends, and he feels obligated to follow through. Herod is depicted as a weak, impulsive man who wants to save face in front of his cohorts more than he wants to do the honorable thing and spare John's life. Thus, John is martyred for speaking the truth about the royal family.

In Matthew, Herodias's story is sandwiched between a series of parables spoken by Jesus and the healing and feeding of the five thousand (Matt.

13–14). In both Mark and Matthew, Jesus is not directly involved in the story. In both accounts, the name of Herodias's daughter is not given. In both, it is Herodias's desire to see John dead.

In Mark, the story serves as a critique of the wicked royal court. There are already problems in Herod's administration. For the average citizen, Herod is a man who should be watched. His decisions are suspect. Anything he does that will be displeasing to God will further undermine his authority. Herod does not want to kill John because he respects him. But his own ego will not permit him to make a decision not to kill the prophet.

A clash of powers in this story is reminiscent of Jezebel's problems with Elijah. John's message was that the powers of this world are evil and will be destroyed. This story only confirms that view. Herod has the power to change his mind and change the course of history. But in a drunken and ego- tistical move, he carries out a plan that he knows is wrong. Despite his respect for John, Herod gives in to the weakness of his ego and sense of honor. Herodias represents the woman of status who undermines the inno- cent hero (remember Potiphar's wife and Joseph?). Herodias is the danger- ous, foreign woman.

In Matthew, Herod wants John dead but resists for political reasons: Herod "feared the crowd, because they regarded John as a prophet" (Matt. 14:5). Herod is afraid the people might rebel and bring further dissension upon his administration. Matthew, too, highlights the struggle of God's chosen against the powers of this world. In both Mark and Matthew, John is the innocent victim of a ruler who has no morals or ethics. Both are sacri- ficed for the movement of God's will in the world.

In some ways, Herodias is portrayed as a trickster. She uses her limited power to change the outcome of events. She is characterized as a vengeful, heartless, determined woman. Her status as Herod's wife is not to be ignored. Like Jezebel, Herodias grew up in the palace (her grandfather was Herod the Great). And she was used to royal prerogatives. Beyond this brief portrait, we know just a little more about her. She sought political advancement for her husband. Instead, he was banished, and she had the option of going with him or maintaining her freedom. She chose to go into exile with her husband. Her decision may have indicated genuine love and affection for him—she gave up her life to be with him and live as outcasts.

In the Christian Scriptures, the picture of Herodias is negative. She holds on to her anger until she gets what she wants. She drags her daughter into the fray and uses her to achieve her ends. She is a stark contrast to John the Baptist, who is righteous and holy. She is manipulative and vindictive; John is innocent and moral. She may have looked at John the way Jezebel looked at Naboth— according to royal protocol, neither men had the authority or the right to oppose the ruler. Both men were guilty of insubordination. We do not see her in any other setting, so we do not know what was important to her.

We have seen in earlier studies how family dysfunction continues until the cycle is broken. We can imagine Herodias as a spoiled woman who learned how to be ruthless by watching her family in action.

What if the picture we have of her is unfair and distorted? Although she was a woman of status, she had no real power to implement anything. At best, she could influence her husband; at worst, she could suffer in silence. She is deemed evil because she caused the death of John the Baptist. But we never get to see her as a person. We do not know what the people may have been saying about her behind her back. How did she handle the gossip and snickers of those who never bothered to hear her side of the story concerning her marriage? Her anger toward John conveyed that she was a passionate woman. She was a mother to a young daughter. What was the quality of their interactions? She cared about her husband—what was the quality of their interactions? She cared about what others thought of her—does that make her selfish? She was ambitious—how would her life have been different had she been able to play a public leadership role?

What we find in Herodias is a family history of pain and abuse. She was a strong woman with strong passions and opinions. She was caring, determined, focused, smart, and patient. In another world and in another time, who knows to what heights she may have risen? She saw opportunity when it presented itself and was quick to take action. Instead, the implied message of the text is that Herodias should leave public life to the men and keep herself in the house doing "women" things.

Much of our perception about Herodias and her daughter stems from Richard Strauss's opera entitled *Salomé*. It is here that Herodias's daughter is named. Both she and Herodias are portrayed as seductive women who use their sensuality for evil and wicked purposes. Herod is portrayed as a lecherous old man who desires his stepdaughter. In the opera, Salomé dances seductively with the use of seven veils that induce Herod to make the ill-fated oath that chops off John the Baptist's head. The opera embellishes the story greatly and we are influenced by it. Both in the opera and in the Bible, we are left with a horrible picture of Herodias.

Herodias is representative of women who have strong opinions and express them in angry ways. The intensity of the grudge would indicate something more than John's condemnation of her marriage. Scripture does not give us a full enough portrait of Herodias for a true assessment of her personality and character. Her life must have had areas of unfulfillment. The emptiness of her life must have caused her great pain.

Today, some women are accused of having bad attitudes. These women always seem angry and uptight. They complain constantly and never see anything positive. They hardly ever smile or put on a pleasant face for the world. We are uncomfortable around them and are exasperated in our attempts to help them see the good in things. Perhaps Herodias was a woman with an attitude problem. Perhaps she was so obsessed with getting John the Baptist that others did not want to spend much time with her.

It is likely that we all know someone who makes us uncomfortable. We are annoyed by people who make us listen to their tales of woe. We tune them out when they start talking about their aches and pains. We are frustrated with those who dominate conversations with their issues when we have things we want to say, too. In many ways, our society has lost the fine art of conversation—the give-and-take of communication where each is truly heard. We often greet people with "How are you?" but rarely stop long enough to hear the answer. We are like ships passing in the night, barely acknowledging each other's presence.

Herodias may have been a woman who needed the support of friends. She may have needed friends to tell her to let her obsession with John go. She may have needed friends to help her move on. Herodias is a mirror for myriads of people who are lonely and lost. These days, we pay counselors, psychologists, and psychiatrists huge sums of money just to listen to us. Phone services—psychic hot lines, dating services, and chat lines—are making tons of money because many people are just looking for someone to talk with.

Too many people turn to drugs or alcohol or food to avoid dealing with their problems. It is easier to escape than it is to face reality. Who knows what kind of person Herodias could have been had there been opportunities to deal with her problems? Some of us may be indulging unhealthy habits because we do not know what else to do. Abundant resources are available to us, but we hesitate to use them. We do not want to appear weak or out of control. But we live in a complex time. We have too much to do with too little time and too little energy. Our days speed by in a blur; we have to look at our calendars just to remember what we did last week. Many of us have not had a day off (a real day off) or vacation in years.

Many of us do not know how to relax. Most of us do not know how to play. So the stress and pressure and tension build. One day we suddenly realize our breathing is shallow, our bodies are tense, and we do not know why. It is important in the hectic world in which we live to take time to relax, to recharge our batteries, to spend quality time with people who make us feel good.

We have the impression that for Herodias, these were luxuries that even a princess found rare. She might have let the thing with John the Baptist go if she had other and important things to do. We can see that she has some positive traits: she is patient, resourceful, and passionate. She is determined, focused, and loyal. She clearly has leadership qualities, but they are wasted.

We will never know the truth about her. Instead of presenting a three-dimensional human being, the Gospel writers have given us a caricature of the evil and scorned woman. Behind the mask may lurk a misunderstood, frustrated woman with no outlets for her creative energies. Let us learn a lesson from Herodias!

REFLECTION QUESTIONS

1. In what ways are you like Herodias? Explain.
2. What do you do to relax? How often? Is this enough? Be specific.
3. Have you ever been a victim of unfair gossip? Do you engage in gossip? Why?
4. Discrimination results when one group unfairly uses its power over another group. What are appropriate ways of handling power and privilege?
5. What advice do you think Jezebel would offer Herodias?
6. Herodias could never escape her family history because of her name. What does your name say about you? Do you wish you had another name? What would it be? Why?
7. Do you hold grudges? What can you do to change this habit?
8. How do you handle your anger? Are there other ways of dealing with anger? Explain.
9. John the Baptist is described as righteous and holy. Do such people exist today? Who are they? What makes them so?
10. What can you do to cheer up someone? Will you do it? Why or why not?
11. How do you react to random acts of kindness? Explain.

11

THE WOMAN CAUGHT IN ADULTERY:
FALLEN OR FORGIVEN?

The Gospel of John is the fourth Gospel. It is different enough from Matthew, Mark, and Luke to be labeled "asynoptic." The Synoptic Gospels, which give similar pictures of Jesus and share much of the same information, are alike in outline, content, time frame, and wording. John's Gospel is filled with different images and ideas. John comes at Jesus' identity and mission from a different perspective. John establishes Jesus' identity early on by linking him to God's creative process (John 1:1–5). Jesus engages in long conversations about Mosaic law and its interpretation; the D tradition reflects this concern for the instructions given to Moses on Mount Sinai. We have here a continuation of themes developed in the Hebrew Scriptures as well as concerns that have surfaced in earlier studies.

Jesus is shown in conflict with the scribes and Pharisees, the Jewish leaders of the day. They are constantly "testing" Jesus in order to indict him. They ask Jesus in various situations to interpret the law—they try to put Jesus in a no-win situation. His answer could be the difference between life and death. If Jesus supports Mosaic law, he can be tried and convicted for treason against the Roman authorities. If he goes against Mosaic law, he can be tried and convicted for blasphemy against God. Despite their efforts, Jesus repeatedly outwits them. A case in point is the story of the woman caught in adultery.

The story of this unnamed woman is found in John 8:2–11. There is some question about where this story fits into the larger Gospel. Some early manuscripts either omit it or place it somewhere else in the Gospel. Some commentators suggest that although this story is a real incident in the ministry of Jesus, it may not have belonged to this Gospel at all.

This woman is one of many unnamed persons in the Gospels who are known by their condition or sin. She is the woman caught in adultery. Two others are the bent-over woman and the woman with the issue of blood. This woman has no name and very little voice. Yet she plays an important role in helping us to understand Jesus and the powers over against which he stood.

Jesus is at the Temple teaching the crowd. The scribes and Pharisees interrupt his lesson. They are dragging a disheveled woman whom they have caught in the act of committing adultery. They make her stand before Jesus as they pose a question to him: "'Teacher, this woman was caught in the very act of committing adultery. Now in the law Moses commanded us to stone such women. Now what do you say?' They said this to test him, so that they might have some charge to bring against him" (John 8:4–6).

You will remember from earlier studies that the penalty for adultery was stoning. Two witnesses were needed to verify the offense. However, according to the D tradition, both partners were to be punished. The leaders have made their plot to trick Jesus much too obvious. In the first place, they have captured only the woman. Where is the man, her partner in crime? To be faithful to Mosaic law, they should have dragged the man along with the woman: "If a man is caught lying with the wife of another man, both of them shall die, the man who lay with the woman as well as the woman. So you shall purge the evil from Israel" (Deut. 22:22).

In the second place, they have not produced two witnesses. If they caught her in the very act, where are the witnesses to verify the charge? It is their word against the woman's word. For all Jesus knows, they may have falsely accused the woman in order to propel their plan to snare him. Without the proper witnesses, they have no case: "A single witness shall not suffice to convict a person of any crime or wrongdoing in connection with any offense that may be committed. Only on the evidence of two or three witnesses shall a charge be sustained" (Deut. 19:15).

Jesus sees through their little plan and refuses to play along. He is not going to give them the fuel they need to destroy him. They ask Jesus a direct question, and he refuses to answer: "Jesus bent down and wrote with his finger on the ground. When they kept on questioning him, he straightened up and said to them, 'Let anyone among you who is without sin be the first to throw a stone at her.' And once again he bent down and wrote on the ground" (John 8:6–8).

Jesus does not engage them on their level. If a debate is to take place, Jesus will do so at the level he determines. Jesus changes the basis of the debate by holding them accountable to the law. Jesus does not deny the ancient punishment—he tells the men to go ahead and throw the first stone, but only if they are innocent of sin. Jesus has cleverly turned their trap back on them. If any man throws a stone, he is the one guilty of blasphemy, for no one is without sin. They are trapped in their own sanctimonious trick.

Imagine their sense of defeat. They really think they have him this time. They probably rejoiced in their "good fortune" to find this woman whom they can use as a scapegoat to get the dreaded Jesus. They feel that Jesus is undermining orthodox Judaism with his emphasis on human beings rather than strict adherence to the laws of Moses. And now their plan has been thwarted and exposed—again! To make matters worse, Jesus does not engage in open confrontation with them. He simply makes a statement and bends back down to write. Jesus has challenged them to think about their ways of seeing the world. The Mosaic law was not designed to be a trap for persons struggling to do good things and be good people. The laws were to govern community life characterized by justice and compassion. These men show no compassion for this woman. They show no concern for her at all. She is handy, and so they attempt to use her. Jesus throws their callousness back at them. Jesus has effectively shut them up and dismissed them. The men are stunned!

In the meantime the woman is silent. We can only imagine what she must have been feeling. She stands before the great teacher who has a reputation of forgiving sins and making people, even women, feel important and valuable. But she stands before him guilty of a serious crime. Even though the scribes and Pharisees present a sloppy case, we can presume that she is guilty. We do not know in what condition they present her before Jesus. Is she fully dressed? Is she half-dressed? How does she feel about being shamed in such a public way—at the Temple? This scene hauntingly echoes the actions of Hosea against Gomer. The woman, no doubt scared out of her wits, has no choice but to stand accused while the men determine her fate. After a while, in the silence, Jesus stands up and deals with the woman. "When they heard it, they went away, one by one, beginning with the elders; and Jesus was left alone with the woman standing before him. Jesus straightened up and said to her, 'Woman, where are they? Has no one condemned you?' She said, 'No one, sir.' And Jesus said, 'Neither do I condemn you. Go your way, and from now on do not sin again'" (John 8:9–11).

None of the men can condemn the woman—no one is without sin. When Jesus addresses the woman, he acknowledges her personhood. The scribes and Pharisees see her as an object to be used to their devious ends. She is not a person in their eyes. Jesus lets her know that despite her sin, she is a human being and is worthy of due respect. He does not launch into a sermon about the evils of adultery. He does not question her about her actions. He does not badger her about being careless enough to get caught. He does not make her feel worse than she already does. He does not further humiliate her. He does not pick up a stone to hit her. He wants to know where her accusers are, and he wants her to know that she is out of danger. The men with the stones are gone. She gets a reprieve—this time. The Greek word translated "condemn" (*katakrino*) is from a root word (*krino*) that implies "separation" or "break." Jesus tells the woman he does not separate or break her off from the rest of the community. She is not cast out. She remains part of a community that also knows sin. If her accusers cannot condemn her, neither will Jesus.

Jesus recognizes and acknowledges that she has sinned. He does not forgive her sin, but he gives her another chance. She is free to live another day.

She is able to choose. She has the opportunity to start anew. She knows that she is guilty, but she is alive and can repent of her sin. She can return to her husband and begin the challenge of reconciling with him.

We saw in the Hebrew Scriptures that sexual sins garnered harsh punishment. Jesus does not make sexual sins any worse than others. We do not know what sins the men were guilty of—whatever they were, the sin of the woman was not greater. Jesus seems to be saying that sin is sin.

Popular interpretations of this story focus on the grace of forgiveness the woman receives. Her sin has not been counted against her, and Jesus gives her a fresh start. However, we do a disservice to the text if we let the scribes and Pharisees off the hook. The religious leaders of the people have gone to great lengths to entrap Jesus. Patriarchy rears its ugly head once again. The men in this story do not care about this woman. If the leaders are willing to sacrifice this woman, what kind of servants are they for God? How can they be expected to usher in God's reign of justice, peace, compassion, and love? The men are eager to execute Jesus on religious grounds. But they embody the sermons of the prophets of the Hebrew Scriptures—they give lip service to the will of God, but they are not able to fulfill it. They use the obligations of the covenant to beat people into submission or to kill them. And, of course, women bear the brunt of the abuse. In challenging the scribes and Pharisees, Jesus challenges the very essence of their practiced religion and patriarchal worldview.

This woman, caught in adultery, symbolizes more than Jesus' gracious mercy, although she certainly symbolizes that. She also symbolizes Jesus' ministry that challenges institutions that are taken for granted. He shows that there is a different way of seeing and being in the world. He does not curse anyone, he does not engage in verbal sparring, he does not get physical—he simply turns the people's convictions back on them. He forces them to think about what they are doing. Through his actions, Jesus has made possible the redemption of all the parties involved. The men can begin to think in new categories that are concerned for and focused on the humanity of the other citizens. The woman can rethink her actions, repent, and live a life free of the sin of adultery.

This woman represents all of us who have sinned and stand guilty. Through the ages, society has found ways to embarrass and humiliate its people. I am reminded of Nathaniel Hawthorne's classic novel *The Scarlet Letter*, where Hester Prynne is forced to wear the emblem of shame, while her partner moves in anonymity. In some countries, people's crimes dictate their punishment; a thief, for instance, will have a hand cut off. The woman caught in adultery is known only for her sin. She has no name, no identity apart from her action. We wonder how her husband will react to her public humiliation and abuse. We wonder how her girlfriends will react to her now. We wonder what she will say to her children. We wonder how she will hold her head up, knowing that everyone knows her scandal.

The woman caught in adultery is the victim of a group of men who were out to get Jesus. The law was supposed to provide fair and just treatment for those who transgressed. In this instance, the woman alone is left to bear the burden for the act. She has no way to hold her adulterous partner accountable to the law. The system that promised fairness has not worked for this woman in this situation. Instead, the law is used against her and she is helpless to oppose her treatment by the leaders who have brought her before Jesus to be judged.

Women throughout the world find themselves victimized by men in power. Many women have few resources to fight the injustice of systems that favor men. They are left to suffer in silence. There are countless stories of women who are told to work within "the system" only to have that system betray them. For instance, some health care providers do not cover the cost of mammograms or pap smears despite the clear evidence that these examinations save lives. Pharmaceutical companies test drugs for safety but fail to include women in clinical trials. Women are castigated for increasing the welfare rolls, but the welfare departments claim not to have the resources to find deadbeat dads and make them pay child support. Women are encouraged to take jobs to support their children, but affordable child care is unavailable. Conditions for some women are improving, but too many remain hopeless and helpless.

There is much in our society that dehumanizes people. Our attitudes may too often make people feel unworthy and valueless. We sometimes make people feel unimportant and bothersome. Jesus brings a new message that things do not have to be this way. Jesus allows us to stand before him. In the silence, he challenges us to new visions about how we can and should function as human beings. The scribes and Pharisees did a great injustice to the woman in this story. They made her think of herself only in terms of her sin. Jesus presented an alternative. Because she stood silent before Jesus, she could think of herself as a human being, not perfect, but worthy of respect. She stood silent before Jesus, and he gave her—and he gives us—a second chance!

ℛEFLECTION QUESTIONS

1. The scribes and Pharisees engage in a double standard by presenting only the woman for punishment. In what ways is the double standard operative today?

2. How do you rank sin? Are some sins worse than others? Would Jesus agree with your assessment?

3. Are you surprised that Jesus does not forgive her sin? Why do you think he did not?

4. Should the woman have been punished for her sin? What would be a suitable punishment? What should happen to her partner in sin?

5. The primary goal of the scribes and Pharisees was not to stone the woman. They wanted Jesus. Have you ever been used by someone? How did you handle the situation? What would you do differently if you had the chance?

6. Have you ever been publicly embarrassed? How did you handle this situation? Have you ever embarrassed someone? Why did you do it?

7. Have you ever feared for your life? What did you do? What do you wish you had done?

8. Some people feel they are innocent until they get caught. What is your opinion about this attitude?

9. Have you ever been in a no-win situation? How did you handle it?

10. If you stood silent before Jesus, what would he write in the dirt about you? What would he say to you?

11. Some of us throw stones at others by gossiping about them or mocking or shaming them. What stones do you throw at yourself?

12. For what do you need to be forgiven? How can you claim the forgiveness you seek?

13. Whom do you need to forgive? What prevents you from forgiving that person (or those persons)?

14. What can we do to make public institutions more accountable and humane?

12

SAPPHIRA: GOOD INTENTIONS OR BAD ENDS?

The Acts of the Apostles is the fifth book in the Christian Scriptures and serves as a kind of companion to the Gospel of Luke. Popular interpretation sees Acts as the historical account of the early Christian church from the resurrection of Jesus to Paul's missionary work in Rome. The book focuses particularly on the ministries of Peter and Paul. Acts is not strictly historical, however. There are chronicles and accounts of the apostles' movements and the early days of the church. But the book also deals with theological issues and broader social and political issues, and it provides some biographical information.

The first half of the book is concerned with the church at Jerusalem. We get glimpses of the church's leaders and the issues and challenges the church faces. There are a number of themes in the book of Acts: the relationship between Judaism and Christianity; the relationship between Gentile and Jewish Christians; the relationship between the church and Roman authorities.

The story of Sapphira is intertwined with that of her husband, Ananias. This is another puzzling and confusing story. Sapphira and Ananias are members of the early Christian church at Jerusalem. They are struck dead for withholding moneys from the common fund. This story is extremely difficult because it is not clear what crime they committed. This seems to be a case where the punishment does not fit the crime. We will be left with haunting questions, but interesting tidbits tweak our imaginations.

The members of the Christian church at Jerusalem had decided to pool their resources for the common good. The people sold their properties and contributed the proceeds to a common fund, which the apostles administered. This arrangement symbolized the utopian Israelite community where things were shared: "There will, however, be no one in need among you, because God is sure to bless you in the land that your God is giving you as a possession to occupy, if only you will obey your God by diligently observing this entire commandment that I command you today" (Deut. 15:4–5).

One man is lifted up as a proud example of generosity and commitment: Joseph, a Levite native of Cyprus, also known as Barnabas, sold a field and brought the entire proceeds to the apostles for the common pot. We are tipped off that something strange will happen; the very next sentence begins with the word "But." This is how we are introduced to Ananias and his wife, Sapphira: "But a man named Ananias, with the consent of his wife Sapphira, sold a piece of property; with his wife's knowledge, he kept back some of the proceeds, and brought only a part and laid it at the apostles' feet" (Acts 5:1–2).

Of immediate interest is that Ananias seems to have a good relationship with his wife. He consults her before conducting business. She presumably has an equal say in decisions concerning their household. We do not know much about them because no family history is given. We are not told whether they are natives of Jerusalem or another city. We do not know if they have children. They seem to enjoy a good marriage based on mutual respect and consideration. We presume that they are well off financially. There is no indication that they sold all of their land, only a piece of what they owned. Their actions mirror those of Barnabas—they sell something and lay the proceeds at the feet of the apostles. The difference here is that Ananias holds back a portion of the money. Somehow, his deed is known. (Read Acts 5:3–5.)

Peter knows of Ananias's deception and questions him. Peter speaks of Satan, who is different from the *satan* we met in the story about Job's wife. Here Satan, or the devil, represents the forces of evil that influence people to sin. It was believed by some that the devil was responsible for illnesses of various kinds and tragic natural phenomena. Satan has some power, but this power does not equal God's. Satan may delay God's plans but cannot thwart them forever.

Peter accuses Ananias of allowing Satan to fill his heart and fashion a deed of hypocrisy. Peter reminds Ananias that the land was his to do with as he wanted. He was under no legal obligation to give all the proceeds to the common fund. All he had to do was to be honest about his contribution. In a way, Ananias was cheating on his taxes and thought he could get away with it. Peter convicts Ananias for trying to cheat God. It is not clear whether God kills Ananias or whether Ananias is so shamed and filled with remorse that he dies under the strain. At any rate, Ananias dies on the spot.

We are told that great fear grips all who hear of Ananias's deed and death. He is carried out and buried. The Greek word translated "fear" (*phobos*) is from a root word implying a comprehensive fright resulting in awe or apprehension. Those who hear of Ananias will be moved to be really careful about their conduct.

Later, Sapphira comes in and is confronted by Peter, just as her husband has been:

> After an interval of about three hours his wife came in, not knowing what had happened. Peter said to her, "Tell me whether you and your husband sold the land for such and such a price." And she said, "Yes, that was the price." Then

Peter said to her, "How is it that you have agreed together to put the Spirit of God to the test? Look, the feet of those who have buried your husband are at the door, and they will carry you out." (Acts 5:7–9)

Sapphira suffers the same fate as her husband. Peter does not remind her that the land was hers to do with as she pleased. She is accused of conspiring with her husband to test the Spirit of God. "Immediately she fell down at his feet and died. When the young men came in they found her dead, so they carried her out and buried her beside her husband" (Acts 5:10).

This story raises interesting questions. We are not sure why Ananias and Sapphira held back money from the proceeds while pretending to donate the entire amount. They were obviously well-to-do. Some commentators speculate that they wanted the attention that sacrificial giving would bring them. They wanted to be praised by others in the congregation and recognized for the generosity of their gift.

The narrator tells us that the church was of one heart and soul; no one claimed private ownership of any possessions (Acts 4:32). Yet the action of Ananias and Sapphira shows that the early church was not perfect. At least some persons in the church had not totally committed themselves to communal life. Peter goes on to say that persons retained the right to hold on to their possessions. There was no legal obligation or penalty for private ownership. So Ananias and Sapphira's actions are puzzling.

Further, it is not clear why Ananias and Sapphira made separate appearances in front of the apostles. If they had made a joint decision about how much to contribute, why did they not make it together? There is no indication that Sapphira would have been prevented from accompanying her husband because of her gender.

We note that Sapphira had no idea what had happened to her husband. In the period of three hours, word had not reached her that she was a widow. Where were her friends? Why was she uninformed? Where was she for three hours, and what was she doing? Was she shopping with the money they withheld?

An important element in the book of Acts is the work and presence of the Holy Spirit. The Holy Spirit carried out the work Jesus had given before his crucifixion. The Holy Spirit carried out God's mission until the apostles were anointed. The Holy Spirit gave birth to the early church—the early church was a Spirit-filled congregation. It has been suggested that the crime of Ananias and Sapphira was not withholding money or lying to the apostles. Their crime was in their refusal or inability to see the church as a community born in and led by the Spirit. As such, their attempt at deception was a crime against the Spirit—symbolic of Satan's opposition to God. They had allowed themselves to be used by Satan; they had forgotten whose they were. They belonged to the risen Christ, not the devil. If the new church was going to thrive, it needed honest commitment from its members. The sin of hypocrisy could not be tolerated, so punishment was swift and sure.

Another issue has to do with the severity of the punishment. It is difficult to think of a God who would just strike someone dead. Commentators suggest that Ananias and Sapphira behaved like individuals in a context of people striving to be community—of one heart and soul. Neither Ananias nor Sapphira had an opportunity to defend or explain himself or herself. Ananias never said a word. Sapphira spoke only to incriminate herself. This story is similar to that of Achan in Joshua 7. Achan kept some of the "devoted things" after the Israelite victory over Jericho. God had commanded that all the spoils from the battle be destroyed. Because of Achan's sin, Joshua suffered a military setback at the city of Ai. After Achan confessed, he and his family were stoned to death. One man put the entire community in jeopardy.

Being well off, Ananias and Sapphira were more than likely to have been generous already in their giving to the church. They walked the streets of Jerusalem and encountered the beggars. They were active members of the church; they knew the needs of the widows and orphans. There is no indication that they had been stingy in previous days. Why would they now choose to withhold?

Some commentators suggest that this story is designed to make a point. Those who heard this story were amazed and in awe of a God who avenged deception against God's own Spirit. Members were free to make their own choices. But for the sake of community, their choices must be based on truth, not hypocrisy. Members would be reminded of Jesus' teaching that one could not serve mammon and God. The early church called for a decision—one could not straddle the fence. In the stories we studied from the Hebrew Scriptures, a major theme is the importance of total devotion and service to the one true God. Things have not changed—God still requires complete devotion and service. The difference is that Jesus has now shown the way.

In the matter of Ananias and Sapphira, each paid the consequence for the joint decision. They knowingly and deliberately tried to deceive the apostles with their partial gift. For that, they should have been held accountable. Ananias has been dismissed as a weak man. Sapphira has been accused of being greedy and selfish. She is expected, by some, to have prevented her husband from holding back the proceeds from the property. We are not told whose idea it was to keep the money. Ananias did not speak. Did his silence mean he was a passive husband who was manipulated by his aggressive, evil wife?

Sapphira was a strong woman who was an equal partner in her marriage. She had some understanding of economics and money management. She was forthright; she did not hem or haw when confronted by Peter. She and her husband had agreed on the amount they would give—that was her story and she stuck to it. She knew what she was doing and owned up to her actions. And we know what happens to these women! The narrator awards her equal status with her husband, and she suffered the same fate. In the early church, women will be held as accountable as men for their choices and decisions. We do not know to which partner the land belonged. Was the land his or hers? Was it land that they obtained after their marriage? We do not know. We do know that Sapphira was a woman with a name and a head for numbers. She was loyal and devoted to her husband. She was an active member of a growing church. She enjoyed a measure of independence. Despite her sudden demise, she remains as a sign of the potential changing role of women.

Sapphira would represent people who seek getting something for nothing. These people want to reap big rewards without expending much time or energy. They think they can pull something over on the system. They may prosper for a while, but their past usually catches up with them. They usually pay a price for trying to manipulate or deceive others for their own selfish ends. It is not always clear what motivates these people. They feel that the system owes them something—*why* is the mystery. They may be frustrated with a philosophy that makes hard work the requisite for rewards. But for some, hard work is just that—hard work, drudgery, boredom, and frustration. For these people, there is no way except through some kind of miracle.

We do not know what motivated Sapphira and Ananias to hold back some of their resources. They came from a situation where fortunes were tenuous or elusive. They may have thought that the new church was corrupt—why should they give their all to something they were not sure about? They wanted to keep a little in a nest egg—just in case! Many of us think about having a little money for a rainy day; it is good to have a little something stashed away in case of an emergency.

Some of us are heavy consumers. We like things and spend large sums of money to have the latest electronic gadgets. We accumulate stuff because we think it makes us happy. In our quest for bigger and better things, in our quest to keep up with the Joneses, we eventually realize that the things we have do not satisfy the hunger of our souls.

Sapphira and Ananias had a grand opportunity to show the world a different way of life. They had the opportunity to show that there really is plenty for everybody on this earth. They had the opportunity to show that hunger is not a given in our world. They had the opportunity to show that widows and orphans could live better than second-class citizens. They had the opportunity to show how Jesus has made a difference. Instead, they clung to old behaviors that said, "If I give all I have, I won't have enough for myself." The new church at Jerusalem was an experiment in an alternative lifestyle—real community with plenty for all because no one had more than was necessary. The experiment was shaky from the beginning. We continue to struggle with what is the right balance between too much and just enough. As long as there are hungry and homeless people in the world, we have work to do. As long as there are sick and lonely people in the world, we have work to do. As long as there are poor people in the world, we have work to do.

In the face of human need and ecological disaster, we are filled with fear and awe. May we use these feelings as fuel to do the work that God and Jesus and the Holy Spirit have for us!

REFLECTION QUESTIONS

1. It is not clear from the story how Sapphira and Ananias died. If God killed them, what image of God is portrayed in this story? Did God overact in this story? Explain.

2. What is the image of the apostle Peter in this story? What does this say about church leadership?

3. It has been suggested that the deaths of Ananias and Sapphira are the result not of God's vengeance but of God's divine justice. What is the difference between the two?

4. What are Sapphira's strengths? Is there a little of Sapphira in you? Explain.

5. What is the role of forgiveness for those who lie and cheat?

6. Ananias and Sapphira agreed to lie about the money. What does this say about their marriage?

7. Have you ever pretended to be better off than you are? Why?

8. What are the characteristics of true Christian community? Have you experienced this kind of community?

9. What prevents people from being honest? What can they do about it?

10. How would you spend a million dollars? Explain your motivation.

11. How do you feel about money? Do you have enough? What would be too little?

12. How can a congregation hold its members financially accountable? How should a congregation discipline its members?

$\mathcal{M}$y motivation for writing this book was to find ways to preach about women that did not make them villains or victims. I wanted to expand the list of women who provide positive role models and serve as inspiration for modern Christians. Through my exploration of the stories of some "bad girls," I have found persons who have something of value to say to us. Most stories in the Bible about women have been distorted to suit a male-oriented worldview. With each of our bad girls, we have wrestled with issues of cultural difference, power, sexuality, spirituality, and creativity. We have meditated on women who had power; took risks to accomplish their goals; put themselves in jeopardy; moved from powerlessness to security, however they defined it; and had gumption and courage.

No doubt you already have ideas about how to teach and preach the stories of these women. The ongoing challenge is to make the stories accessible to the church, and to incorporate them into the teaching and preaching that already happen. I hope the reflection questions have stimulated some thinking about how these stories can be used in the life and mission of the church. I offer the following possibilities as you seek ways to make these stories a part of our church life.

Job is often the subject of sermons about faith. He is presented as a perfect example of faith under fire and his wife is portrayed as one who has no faith. To counterbalance unfair treatment of her, I presented Mrs. Job's story as an opportunity to explore the issue of doubt in faith development. The theme for the sermon was that throughout life, with its ups and downs, we can depend on God to be a constant presence. Using Job 2:1–10, I outlined the following points for the sermon:

➤ Bad things happen to all of us; no one is exempt from unexplainable and unexpected events and conditions.
➤ Mrs. Job is a product of her culture—she believes, like others in her day, that bad things happen only to bad people and only good things happen to good people. Many of us today believe the same thing: if we do the right things, only good things should happen to us.
➤ Her faith does not make room for the possibility that sometimes things just happen.
➤ Mrs. Job asks the question we all have asked at one time or another: why me? Her question reflects that she understands that experiences—both positive and negative—determine our faith stance. Only people of faith can ask the question. Doubt presupposes belief.

➤ She asks the right question of Job. Her conclusion is faulty—she under-estimates the power of evil in the world; she thinks of God as a capricious giver and withholder of gifts and blessings; she thinks death is the only answer to unexplained ongoing suffering.

➤ Her question sets the tone for the rest of the book of Job; she is on to something that does not get resolved until the end of the book.

➤ Mrs. Job's thinking is flawed; but she, as a person of faith, is not—we cannot condemn her for asking the right question. We can learn from her conclusion and from Job's response to it.

➤ Throughout the adventure and journey of life, God is with us. God does not always deliver us or make things pleasant; sometimes God gives us what we need to make it through whatever hardship is present.

➤ Faith development happens in the face of hardships and our ability to survive them. Without such experiences, we are like robots, with a superficial and unthinking allegiance to a God who may or may not protect us. True faith comes from going through trauma and surviving.

In this sermon, Mrs. Job becomes a human being who also hurts and doubts. She questions the faithful person's obedience and allegiance—her questions do not diminish God in any way. She is honest and open about how she sees the world and herself in it. Her question leads to a deeper inquiry about life, faith, and God. In this way, she challenges us all to make clear our belief in God.

Few preachers sermonize about Jezebel. When they do, they usually follow the old line: she is evil personified and her character deserves to be condemned. She becomes the scapegoat for all that is wrong with the world and she is described in negative sexual terms. In an unusual twist, I have used the Jezebel story to preach about pluralism. Using 1 Kings 21, I set forth the theme for the sermon: we act out of our cultural understandings and prejudices, and Jesus destroys the barriers we have built to separate ourselves. I made the following points in the sermon:

➤ Jezebel was a Phoenician princess who grew up with royal privilege. Her worldview is shaped by royal prerogative. Thus, Naboth's refusal to sell or exchange the vineyard is in her eyes an act of subordination. He does not have the right to refuse the king. Here we have two cultures clashing.

➤ She is concerned about her husband's depression and acts to make him happy. Her motivations are right, but her tactics are wrong. She does not have Naboth killed for political reasons; she simply wants to make her seemingly passive husband happy.

➤ Jezebel understands enough about Israelite culture to know how she needs to go about the task of obtaining the vineyard for Ahab—she uses the law to get her way. She is acutely aware of the cultural differences; she chooses not to change hers; she uses Naboth's against him.

➤ She does not consider her actions to be wrong; she is simply exercising the power and status conferred upon her by the society.

➤ What Jezebel does is wrong; however, her act is not so different from the ways in which racism is manifested in this society. Many whites ignore the humanity of people of color. White privilege allows whites to build institutions and establish systems that benefit them and leave people of color out. Many whites make only superficial attempts to understand other cultures and people.

➤ The African American civil rights movement was an attempt by blacks in the United States to become visible to the white power structure; it was a movement of the "common folk," who were tired of being ignored and discriminated against. Naboth is not able to protest his innocence because the law worked against him in that instance. African Americans were able to change the legal structures through perseverance and at great cost—including death!

➤ African Americans risked limb and life because they believe in Jesus as liberator. Jesus is the one who makes all people equal regardless of color and nationality. Belief in Jesus makes real the possibility that we can all get along. If Jezebel had had an encounter with Jesus, perhaps she would not have done the callous deed of killing Naboth.

Jezebel's worldview is in sharp contrast with those in Israel. Today, we are dealing with issues of pluralism, diversity, and multiculturalism as we continue to negotiate race relations and as we welcome new immigrants to these shores. Furthermore, we have work to do in extending hospitality to those who have been wronged in the past. In this sermon, Jezebel is not some brazen sexual being, but rather a woman who is insensitive and narrow in her worldview.

These are just two examples of how women's stories can be used in the life of the church. Neither sermon is presented as a women's sermon, but both could be modified to serve that purpose. Stories of biblical women have something to teach us all about the world in which we live. We need only take the time to wrestle with them.

Bad Girls of the Bible is just the start of looking at some of the women in scripture in different, more comprehensive ways. I encourage you to continue your study. We have not heard the last word from these, our sisters. And there are other biblical women waiting for a chance to speak or be noticed. This book ends with a list of resources. Please use them.

I know your ideas will be creative—and I want to know about them! Please write to me and let me know what you are doing, what resources you have discovered, and what you think of this resource. I am available to conduct workshops, retreats, and leadership development training based on this book.

Let me hear from you! My address is:

Rev. Barbara J. Essex
PMB 61
16781 Torrence Ave.
Lansing, IL 60438-6018

*T*his section provides additional information about biblical critical interpretative tools.

There are two major approaches to the study of the Bible: eisegesis and exegesis. "Eisegesis" comes from a Greek word that means "to lead into." That is, one reads into the Bible one's own ideas as if the ideas were God's. Those who eisegete tend to dilute, distort, and misinterpret the biblical message by putting words into God's mouth. Some like to guess what the actions of God will be. Others are afraid to face the truth of the message because it is not what they want to hear. There are a number of ways to eisegete:

➤ *Prooftexting* is taking various verses of scripture out of their original context and placing them together to "prove" some point. Prooftexting ignores the original meaning and purpose of the passage and ignores the who, what, where, and why of the text. This method carries the mistaken notion that each verse is sacred because it is in the Bible. This method negates the big picture of the biblical message.

➤ *Overspiritualizing* is taking passages and references in the Bible that have to do with objects, events, places, and persons in this world and declaring that they have to do with some otherworldly, spiritual unseen realm; this method does not take seriously the incarnation (the birth of Jesus in human flesh) or creation as "good." God moves in the context of history among real people, not in some fuzzy otherworld.

➤ *Allegorizing* states, without scholarly, critical bases, that difficult passages have secret or mystical meanings hidden in an allegory (a narrative story that teaches a lesson or makes a point). The interpreter gives his or her personal interpretation of the assumed allegory. While there are symbolic language and images in God's dealing with human beings, there is a concreteness about God's actions that encourages us to keep one foot on solid ground.

➤ *Literalizing* states that everything written in the Bible must be regarded as literal, historical events and descriptions of concrete objects. This leads to religious fantasy and magical thinking rather than dealing with reality.

Eisegesis leads to faulty biblical interpretation, which leads to "bad" theology, which leads to a faith stance that is inadequate and shaky for helping people to live fully and joyfully. This kind of faith is puny and weak; people fall away from the faith and from the church when they are unable to reconcile the biblical teaching with real life. This method of biblical interpretation is never acceptable from disciples of Christ.

The second approach to biblical study is exegesis. "Exegesis" comes from a Greek word that means "to lead out of." That is, the original and intended meaning of the Bible is allowed to come out and God speaks for God's self. Piety, personal devotion, faith, and commitment are no substitutes for sound exegesis. We are called to use the minds that God has given us in matters of faith, morals, and biblical interpretation. Responsible study is the work of the mind and of the heart. We need the critical use of resources to determine the biblical text, the literary form of the text, the meaning of words and phrases for the original audience of the text, and to understand the text in light of its total background. Some methods of exegesis include the following:

> *Form criticism* is a method of analyzing and interpreting the Bible through a study of its literary types or genres; it examines the structures, intentions, and settings of the biblical texts. This tool answers the questions: Who used a given form? In what context was the form used? For what purpose was the form used? Form criticism deals with the earliest, preliterary phase of Israel's story; that is, we are dealing with the oral traditions before they were written down. The purpose of this tool is to relate the texts to the living people and institutions of ancient Israel by uncovering what was being said by the use of certain forms.

> *Literary criticism* deals with units of the Bible and with the historical settings in which the writing occurred. It answers the question: How does the text hang together? This tool attempts to outline the plan or structure of the text by looking at words and phrases that are repeated and by looking at substitute words and phrases. The work of literary criticism deals with whether a text is written by one person or several, whether literary sources have been used, and whether editors have reworked the text in some way. Literary criticism must relate literary findings to their historical context. To do this, information is needed about the languages, cultures, history, thought forms, and religions of the ancient world.

> *Textual criticism* attempts to recover the original copies of biblical books by comparing existing texts. This tool examines the texts for changes in wording and meaning. Every text is conditioned by its historical situation and stands at a particular point in the process of transmission. The same text will mean different things in different situations. This tool answers the question: What course did the history of the Bible take?

> *Redaction criticism* is concerned with the interaction and connection between a tradition and a later interpretative point of view. This tool looks at how smaller units from the oral tradition or written source were put

together to form larger passages. Redaction criticism tries to uncover the author's or editor's theological motivation by asking: For whom was this tradition written? For what reasons was the tradition written? What situation gave rise to this tradition?

The Yahwist or J tradition is the earliest literary source underlying the first part of the Bible. J is from the German form of Yahweh (Y=J). This tradition is dated from the tenth century B.C.E. (before the common era) and is rooted in the Northern Kingdom (Israel). It displays a positive attitude toward agricultural festivals, the state, and the kingship. It emphasizes the divine initiative that made Israel into a nation. God delivered the Hebrews from slavery in Egypt. This tradition has political interests.

The Elohim or E tradition is from the Northern Kingdom after about 922 B.C.E. The reform in the Northern Kingdom, initiated by Elijah, probably supplied the background for E's reconstruction of Israel's history. E is characterized by its formal, otherworldly tone. E sees complete reliance on God as essential to faithfulness and shows a preference for an idealized desert existence.

D develops the covenant concept emphasized in E; God lovingly elects Israel (as based in J), and the law is Israel's loyal response to this gift from God.

P enhances the role of Aaron from whom the Jerusalem priesthood traced its descent. The final form of the tradition was probably shaped in the exilic period. The Exile provided the background for P's history.

Achtemeier, Paul J., ed. *Harper's Bible Dictionary.* San Francisco: Harper & Row, 1985.

Aland, Kurt, et al., eds. *The Greek New Testament.* 3d ed. New York: United Bible Societies, 1975.

Bellis, Alice Ogden. *Helpmates, Harlots, and Heroes: Women's Stories in the Hebrew Bible.* Louisville: Westminster John Knox Press, 1994.

Berquist, Jon L. *Reclaiming Her Story: The Witness of Women in the Old Testament.* St. Louis: Chalice Press, 1993.

Beyerlin, Walter, ed. *Near Eastern Religious Texts Relating to the Old Testament.* Philadelphia: Westminster Press, 1978.

Bird, Phyllis A. *Missing Persons and Mistaken Identities: Women and Gender in Ancient Israel.* Minneapolis: Fortress Press, 1997.

Boring, M. Eugene. "The Gospel of Matthew: Introduction, Commentary, and Reflections." In *New Interpreter's Bible,* 87–505. Nashville: Abingdon, 1995.

Botterweck, G. Johannes, and Helmer Ringgren, eds. *Theological Dictionary of the Old Testament.* Multiple volumes. Grand Rapids, Mich.: Eerdmans, 1977.

Bright, John. *A History of Israel.* 3d ed. Philadelphia: Westminster Press, 1981.

Bromiley, Geoffrey W. *Theological Dictionary of the New Testament.* Grand Rapids, Mich.: Eerdmans, 1985.

Bronner, Leila Leah. *From Eve to Esther: Rabbinic Reconstructions of Biblical Women.* Louisville: Westminster John Knox Press, 1994.

Buchmann, Christina, and Celina Spiegel, eds. *Out of the Garden: Women Writers on the Bible.* New York: Fawcett Columbine, 1994.

Cartledge-Hayes, Mary. *To Love Delilah: Claiming the Women of the Bible.* San Diego: LuraMedia, 1990.

Day, Peggy L., ed. *Gender and Difference in Ancient Israel.* Minneapolis: Fortress Press, 1989.

Deen, Edith. *All of the Women of the Bible.* New York: Harper & Row, 1983.

Elliger, K., and W. Rudolph, eds. *Biblia Hebraica Stuttgartensia.* Stuttgart: Deutsche Bibelgesellschaft, 1983.

Exum, J. Cheryl. *Fragmented Women: Feminist (Sub)Versions of Biblical Narratives.* Valley Forge, Pa.: Trinity Press International, 1993.

Fewell, Danna Nolan, and David M. Gunn. *Gender, Power, and Promise: The Subject of the Bible's First Story.* Nashville: Abingdon, 1993.

Fretheim, Terence E. "The Book of Genesis: Introduction, Commentary, and Reflections." In *New Interpreter's Bible,* 319–674. Nashville: Abingdon, 1994.

Grant, Jacquelyn. *White Women's Christ and Black Women's Jesus: Feminist Christology and Womanist Response.* Atlanta: Scholars Press, 1989.

Habel, Norman. *Literary Criticism of the Old Testament*. Philadelphia: Fortress Press, 1971.

Holladay, William A. *A Concise Hebrew and Aramaic Lexicon of the Old Testament*. Grand Rapids, Mich.: Eerdmans, 1971.

Hollyday, Joyce. *Clothed with the Sun: Biblical Women, Social Justice, and Us*. Louisville: Westminster/John Knox Press, 1994.

Huwiler, Elizabeth. *Biblical Woman: Mirrors, Models, and Metaphors*. Cleveland: United Church Press, 1993.

Klein, Ralph W. *Textual Criticism of the Old Testament*. Philadelphia: Fortress Press, 1974.

Krentz, Edgar. *The Historical-Critical Method*. Philadelphia: Fortress Press, 1975.

Macrone, Michael. *Brush Up Your Bible*. New York: Cader Books/HarperPerennial, 1993.

Martin, Clarice J. "Biblical Theodicy and Black Women's Spiritual Autobiography." In *A Troubling in My Soul: Womanist Perspectives on Evil and Suffering*, ed. Emilie M. Townes. Maryknoll, N.Y.: Orbis Books, 1993.

Mays, James L., ed. *Harper's Bible Commentary*. San Francisco: Harper & Row, 1988.

Moyers, Bill. *Genesis: A Living Conversation*. New York: Doubleday, 1996.

Murphy, Cullen. "Is the Bible Bad News for Women?" *Wilson Quarterly* 22, no. 3 (summer 1998): 14–33. Washington, D.C.: Woodrow Wilson International Center for Scholars.

Newsom, Carol A. "The Book of Job: Introduction, Commentary, and Reflections." In *New Interpreter's Bible*, 319–637. Nashville: Abingdon, 1996.

Newsom, Carol A., and Sharon H. Ringe, eds. *The Women's Bible Commentary*. Louisville: Westminster/John Knox Press, 1992.

O'Day, Gail. "The Gospel of John: Introduction, Commentary, and Reflections." In *New Interpreter's Bible*, 491–865. Nashville: Abingdon, 1995.

Pearson, Helen Bruch. *Do What You Have the Power to Do: Studies of Six New Testament Women*. Nashville: Upper Room Books, 1992.

Perkins, Pheme. "The Gospel of Mark: Introduction, Commentary, and Reflections." In *New Interpreter's Bible*, 507–733. Nashville: Abingdon, 1995.

Perrin, Norman. *What Is Redaction Criticism?* Philadelphia: Fortress Press, 1969.

Pippin, Tina. "Jezebel Re-Vamped." *Semeia* 69/70: Intertextuality and the Bible, 221–33. Nashville: Society of Biblical Literature, 1995.

Russell, Letty M., ed. *Feminist Interpretation of the Bible*. Philadelphia: Westminster Press, 1985.

Saunders, Ross. *Outrageous Women, Outrageous God: Women in the First Two Generations of Christianity*. Ridgefield, Conn.: Morehouse Publishing, 1996.

Teubal, Savina J. *Hagar the Egyptian: The Lost Tradition of the Matriarchs*. San Francisco: Harper & Row, 1990.

Tolbert, Mary Ann. "Defining the Problem: The Bible and Feminist Hermeneutics." *Semeia* 28: The Bible and Feminist Hermeneutics. Atlanta: Society of Biblical Literature, 1983.

Trible, Phyllis. *Texts of Terror: Literary-Feminist Readings of Biblical Texts.* Philadelphia: Fortress Press, 1984.

Tucker, Gene M. *Form Criticism of the Old Testament.* Philadelphia: Fortress Press, 1971.

Ulanov, Ann Belford. *The Female Ancestors of Christ.* Boston: Shambhala, 1993.

Updike, John. "Can Eve Be Reprieved? Feminist Scholars Take On the Good Book." *New Yorker,* September 14, 1998, 93–97.

Weems, Renita J. *Battered Love: Marriage, Sex, and Violence in the Hebrew Prophets.* Minneapolis: Fortress Press, 1995.

————. *Just a Sister Away: A Womanist Vision of Women's Relationships in the Bible.* San Diego: LuraMedia, 1988.

Winter, Miriam Therese. *Woman Wisdom: A Feminist Lectionary and Psalter on Women of the Hebrew Scriptures,* Part One. New York: Crossroad, 1991.

————. *Woman Word: A Feminist Lectionary and Psalter on Women of the New Testament.* New York: Crossroad, 1990.

Yee, Gale A. "The Book of Hosea: Introduction, Commentary, and Reflections." In *New Interpreter's Bible,* 195–297. Nashville: Abingdon, 1996.

Zimmerli, Walther. *Old Testament Theology in Outline.* Trans. David E. Green. Edinburgh: T. & T. Clark, 1978.